D1241150

TO FREEDOM
CONDEMNED

JEAN-PAUL SARTRE

TO FREEDOM CONDEMNED

A GUIDE TO HIS PHILOSOPHY

By

Justus Streller

Translated and with an introduction by
WADE BASKIN

THE WISDOM LIBRARY

a division of
PHILOSOPHICAL LIBRARY
New York

Distributed to the Trade by
BOOK SALES, INC.
352 Park Avenue South
New York 10, N.Y.

CONTENTS

TRANSLATOR'S INTRODUCTION

If defined loosely (and no rigid definition suits everyone who feels qualified to express an opinion on the subject) as a system of philosophy evolved from the notion that existence is prior to essence, that man is responsible for his actions, and that man's freedom to choose what he will be is both a blessing and a curse, existentialism is probably as old as thought. Yet the much abused word generally suggests to the American reader the name of the French thinker whose literary and philosophical publications first attracted attention from all quarters during the early post-war years. And still today Jean-Paul Sartre stands as the most articulate—and the most prolific—of modern existentialists. Even so, it is probably safe to assume that few readers have taken the trouble to read in its entirety the one work that would allow them to settle once and for all a controversial question: Is the colorful author of the shocking plays and scandalous novels that have popularized existentialism a serious philosopher or an opportunistic charlatan? *Being and Nothingness*, Sartre's main philosophical work, is proof positive of his sincerity and the indispensable clue to all his activities; in it he probed with startling insight the notions that turn up again in all his novels and plays as well as in all his other expository writings. The present volume represents an attempt on the part of the late Dr. Justus Streller to distill and set down in an orderly fashion the substance of Sartre's monumental study of the structure of man's being and of the significance of man's freedom.

Though Sartre is typical in most respects of the modern French intellectual, his adroit omniscience and his varied accomplishments make it impossible for his severest critics to dismiss him as a *littérateur* or even to challenge him on speculative grounds. Educated in Paris, where he was born on June 21, 1905, he takes his place beside an imposing group of French thinkers who, like Descartes and Comte, have not hesitated to break with tradition in following up a new insight. He attended the Lycée de la Rochelle and the Lycée Louis-le-Grand before entering the Ecole Normale Supérieure; there he majored in philosophy and, in 1929, graduated with high honors. He began his teaching career in provincial secondary schools (Laon, Havre) but managed during the same period (1929-34) to travel and study in Egypt, Greece, Italy, and Germany, where he was a *pensionnaire* at the Institut Français. His studies in philosophy introduced him to the work of Edmund Husserl, Martin Heidegger, and Søren Kierkegaard; soon after his return to France (1935), he published his first philosophical works, studies of the imagination and of the emotions. Until he joined the army as a private in 1939, he taught at the Lycée Pasteur at Neuilly. Sent to the Maginot Line, he was captured and held prisoner for several months. Following his repatriation in the spring of 1941, he returned to the Lycée Pasteur. He moved from there to the Lycée Condorcet but soon gave up his post in order to devote all his time to writing.

Always active in the Resistance movement, Sartre managed to continue publishing despite the censors. *Being and Nothingness,* which appeared in 1943, was a real *tour de force* in that it demonstrated the ability of the French to out-speculate the Germans. During the same year Sartre completed *The Flies,* an open condemnation of all forms of tyranny, which somehow eluded the censors in spite of its message. As a result of his fame as a philosopher and his success as a dramatist and novelist (five novels and two plays appeared 1938-45), after World War II ended, Sartre was acclaimed as the undisputed leader of French intellectuals. As the chief existentialist, the uninhibited conversationalist drew crowds to the Café de la Flore, where he was accustomed to write and to relax with his followers. A legendary figure even before his major philosophical work was translated into English, he traveled widely through the United States (1945-46) and lectured at various universities. Since that time he has continued to write indefatigably; he has covered a wide range of subjects, including literature, esthetics, economics, sociology, and politics. His political views have alienated many of his American readers, but alienation has apparently failed to mollify his stand on crucial issues. He now devotes most of his time to editing of the monthly journal which he founded (1946), *Les Temps Modernes*.

Before he undertook to abstract and classify the seminal ideas of Sartre's master work, Dr. Streller published a German translation of its most significant parts. Dr. Streller intended in his exposition of *Being and Nothingness* to draw together related ideas covering a wide range of topics and thereby to provide a concise introduction to the substructure of all of Sartre's fictional works. A comprehensive view of this substructure will contribute to an understanding and appreciation of the novels and dramas on which much of Sartre's fame rests, and which are in turn intended mainly to serve as introductions to or illustrations of his theory of existentialism. Without tergiversation, Dr. Streller guides the reader through Sartre's treatment of the complexities, absurdities, and paradoxes of human existence. By calling attention to certain affinities to Hegel, Heidegger, and Husserl, he brings into focus Sartre's originality—for example, his discovery of the "Look," which as in the legend of Medusa turns to stone (an object) the one who is looked at (the subject). Painstakingly he brings together scattered statements and pinpoints fertile ideas relating to such seemingly disparate topics as bad faith, anguish, transcendence,

9

the Other, consciousness, love, God, death, and freedom. *To Freedom Condemned* is a compact and well-ordered restatement of the essence of Sartre's compendious *Being and Nothingness.*

WADE BASKIN

Southeastern State College

Note

Quotations from Sartre's original text follow in the main the English translation of Professor Hazel E. Barnes (Philosophical Library, 1956). In drawing up definitions for the items in the "Key to Special Terminology," I have also consulted freely Professor Barnes' valuable work.

W.B.

THINGS

Things are exactly what they are and as they are; that is, they possess being-in-itself* and are in themselves. They exist in pure positivity but are also purely contingent—unfounded and without the possibility of having a foundation. They simply *are*. Their being is absolute.

A thing unsatisfied with its existence and desirous of establishing for itself a foundation must become aware of itself through reflection. It must achieve separation from itself. Obviously, however, it can effect a separation only by splitting in two and keeping its parts distinct. This it accomplishes through the instrumentality of nothingness. It follows that a thing in order to be able to reflect on itself and provide for itself a foundation must contain nothingness. Through pure positivity it is transformed into a negativity, into something that contains nothingness. It is no longer in itself, no longer coincident with itself, but only present with respect to itself. It is no longer *in* itself *but* for itself. It is no longer a thing, an *in-itself*; it is a *for-itself*. And the for-itself possesses consciousness; this means that it possesses at the same time freedom and can select ends. Because it selects and pursues ends, the for-itself acquires individuality. It becomes a man. Choosing and pursuing ends is coincident with the emergence of the for-itself.

Things have qualities. For us the most important are their

* Words coined by Sartre or used by him in a special sense are listed in the "Glossary of Special Terms." Tr.

11

coefficients of hostility and their utility. These qualities are obvious if I consider things from the standpoint of the end selected. For depending on whether things hinder or facilitate my reaching the end, I become aware of their coefficients of hostility or of their utility. "The for-itself discovers itself as engaged in being (that is, in being-in-itself), hemmed in by being, threatened by being; it discovers the state of things which surrounds it as the cause for a reaction of defense or attack. But it can make this discovery only because it freely posits the end in relation to which the state of things it makes threatening or favorable."[1] Before the for-itself makes its choice, things seem indifferent, and the for-itself feels lost in their indifference; it feels neglected and chooses an end in order to compel things to unveil their being, to turn toward it their faces. Along with their being, things naturally unveil also their otherness, that is, the fact that they are not the for-itself.

"We are separated from things by nothing *except by our freedom*; it is our freedom which is responsible for the fact that *there are* things with all their indifference, their unpredictability, and their adversity, and for the fact that we are inevitably separated from them; for it is on the ground of nihilation that they appear and that they are revealed as bound one to another."[2] By nihilation is meant our ability to refuse to accept things as they are and to transform them instead into tools which will help us to attain our goal, acquire knowledge, etc. Our freedom to nihilate, however, "adds *nothing* to things."[3]

IN-ITSELF and FOR-ITSELF*

The for-itself (a thing which has to be what it is because it projects itself toward goals, and which therefore is what it still is not and still is not what it is) and the in-itself (a thing that is in itself) "are reunited by a synthetic connection which is nothing other than the for-itself. The for-itself, in fact, is nothing but the pure nihilation of the in-itself; it is like a hole of being at the heart of Being."[1] In other words, it is a nihilation of being at the heart of an individual and particular in-itself.

This nihilation, which determines the reality of the for-itself, is enough to "cause a total upheaval to *happen* to the in-itself. This upheaval is the world."[2] It follows that the for-itself is not independent. It is a non-substantial absolute (an absolute because it uses its freedom to create itself). It depends on the in-itself. It is for that reason always uncertain; its being is never established but always sought after. "The for-itself is always in suspense because its being is a perpetual reprieve. If it could ever join with its being, then the otherness would by the same stroke disappear and along with it possibles (that is, ends), knowledge, the world."[3] Ontologically and essentially, the in-itself takes precedence over the for-itself.

"It is only by making itself for-itself that being can aspire to be the cause of itself."[4] This necessitates a break "with the

---

* Sartre evidently translated Hegel's *Ansich* and *Fürsich* as *en-soi* and *pour-soi*. Tr.

identity-of-being of the in-itself, a withdrawal by being in relation to itself and the appearance of presence to self or consciousness."[5] But consciousness is nihilation of being and "appears therefore as one stage in a progression toward the immanence of causality—*i.e.*, toward being a self-cause. The progression, however, stops there as a result of the insufficiency of being in the for-itself"[6] (only things have plenitude of being). The for-itself is always an abortive struggle to find a cause, to avoid existing any longer without justification and to acquire the value of an in-and-for-itself.

The in-itself can of course "acquire" something only when it *is* presence or consciousness to itself. Here ontology can only declare "that *everything takes place as if* the in-itself in a project to found it-self gave itself the modification of the for-itself. It is up to metaphysics to form the hypotheses which will allow us to conceive of this process as the absolute event (the upsurge of the for-itself) which comes to crown the individual venture which is the existence of being."[7] Metaphysics must also determine whether the first attempt of the in-itself to found itself is to be interpreted as a "malady of being" and whether the for-itself is to be understood "as more profound malady pushed to nihilation."[8]

The in-itself and for-itself are two modalities, two modes of being. "The for-itself without the in-itself is a kind of abstraction; it could not exist any more than a color could exist without form or a sound without pitch and timbre."[9] "Doubtless the for-itself is a nihilation, but as nihilation it is; and is is in *a priori* unity with the in-itself."[10]

Hence being as a unity consisting of in-itself and for-itself is an ideal Being, namely an In-self grounded on and identical to a For-itself; it is therefore the *ens causa sui*, that is, the Being which is its own cause, the absolute and independent Being which the Scholastics called God. Considered from the point of view of this ideal, unrealizable Being, "the real is an abortive effort to attain to the dignity of the self-cause. Everything happens as if the world, man, and man-in-the-world succeeded in realizing only a missing God. Everything happens therefore as if the it-itself and the for-itself were presented in a state of disintegration in relation to an ideal synthesis,"[11] a synthesis which has never occurred but which "is always indicated and always possible."[12]

MAN

Man is a degenerate, degraded thing. He is a thing that seized upon the insolent plan of delving into the condition of its existence. It surrendered its immaculate positivity in exchange for the fateful capacity to be able to say no, to oppose something, to deny, to forbid, to obstruct, to nihilate. This capacity it acquired by implanting in itself nothingness, the root of all negation. Then it could say "I am not that" or "This is not that." The thing acquired consciousness and changed from an in-itself to a for-itself. Along with consciousness it received the questionable gift of freedom, this for-itself could select from its possibilities an end and project itself toward this end. As a result of its choice and its project the for-itself became a man.

Man is the being who brought into the world nothingness and with nothingness the possibility of nihilating something. "But what am I if not a certain internal negation of the in-itself? Without this in-itself which I deny, I should vanish into nothingness."[1]

"We shall never apprehend ourselves except as a choice in

the making. But freedom is simply the fact that this choice is always unconditioned."[2]

"The for-itself in order to choose itself as a person effects the existence of an internal organization which the for-itself surpasses toward itself, and this internal technical organization (for the appropriation of the world or for living in harmony with others, since these processes are the collective property of mankind, of national, professional, and family groups) is his human or national quality."[3]

Since man is descended from things (from lumps of clay into which God breathed: there was a void in which no thing, no in-itself, nothing was; there existed in the thing a place on which nothingness could settle), he participates in the contingency of things, in their fortuitousness, in their non-urgency, in their groundlessness. One characteristic of man is therefore his facticity, that is, the for-itself's necessary connection with the in-itself, which makes it possible for him to assert that he *is* and that he is as he is. Man has *Dasein* ("being-there"), he exists; but he is "cast" there, that is, he not only is but has to be there.

The main employment of man is to recover the being-in-itself of things and all the while be for him-self—not to merge with the world of things but to in-corporate it in himself. His desire is therefore to be in-and-for-itself, to become the proof and foundation of his self (an *ens causa sui*); he wishes to free himself from contingency, that is, to become God.

Christ sacrificed himself in order to bring into being the true man; man destroys himself in his striving after being-in-and-for-itself in order to bring into being God. The true meaning of human behavior therefore transcends egoism, altruism, and disinterest. "Man makes himself man in order to be God,"[4] that is, to become his own foundation. But since "there is no common measure between human reality and the self-cause which it wants to be, one could just as well say that man loses himself in order that the self-cause may exist."[5]

Being-a-man is being-in-the-world, and man can not tear

16

himself away from the world unless he tears himself away from himself. He actually does this in doubt, in interrogation, in suspension of judgment, etc. Here one state of consciousness is wrenched away from another that immediately precedes and motivates it, with the result that a caesura is produced. This caesura is nothingness. Nothingness is impregnable precisely because it is nothing.

As a consequence of his freedom man is always separated by nothingness from what he has just been, that is, from his being. Never can a man's act be explained by what can be asserted about him, for man *is* what he has been. An act, on the contrary, is actual; it anticipates the future and always transcends man's being.

If a man directs his undivided attention toward something and actively gives himself over to it, his conduct has no "outside" (that is, he does not observe it); "it is merely a process of relating the instruments . . . to the end to be attained, a pure mode of losing myself in the world, of causing myself to be drunk in by the things as ink is by a blotter in order that an instrumental complex oriented toward an end may be synthetically detached from the ground of the world."[6]

A man can not actually make himself an object of cognition. An object is what my consciousness is not and what has in itself no trace of consciousness. For outside my own consciouness there is nothing that has for me the characteristics of consciousness. A self that I have made into my object is therefore a self that is not my self. For even if I could see myself clearly and distinctly as an object, what I saw would still not be an adequate representation of what I am in and for myself.

Man's being is tied not only to his being-for-itself but also to his being-for-others. Both the upsurge of my consciousness and the upsurge of my being-for-others have the character of absolute events. My being-for-others is the first fact that I meet with, and the one that I meet with continuously. At all

17

events I must be the one who is *not* something else or the Other. In this negation directed toward myself I bring myself into being, I become my Self and the Other emerges. To produce the Other, my consciousness must have the faculty "not to be" the Other; it must therefore spontaneously wrench itself away from the Other (who "is" my consciousness to begin with) and choose for itself non-being. This non-being is the Other as such. My being-for-myself invests the Other not with being but rather with otherness, the characteristic of being someone besides me. "It is necessary that the other be present to consciousness in every part and even that it penetrate consciousness completely in order that conscious precisely by *being nothing* may escape the Other who threatens to ensnare it. If consciousness were abruptly to be something, the distinction between itself and the Other would disappear at the heart of undifferentiation."[7] The Other is of course (in contrast to things-in-themselves) exactly what I myself am: for-itself and consciousness. He therefore has the same mode of being as I. By excluding the Other he is myself. "The Other exists for consciousness only as a *refused self*,"[8] that is, I exist for myself as the self that has been refused by him, and only as that self. "Thus the Other whom I recognize in order to refuse to be him is before all else the one *for whom my for-itself is*."[9] But I nevertheless refuse to be a self through which the Other can make me into an object (in his judgment, etc.).

"Thus my being-for-others . . . is a perfectly real being, my being as the condition of my selfness confronting the Other and of the Other's selfness confronting me."[10]

Shame, the feeling of man's original fall, results not from the fact that I have committed a particular wrong but simply from the fact "that I have 'fallen' into the world in the midst of things"[11] and must have the help of the Other to overcome objectness and be what I am.

Adam and Eve realized after the fall that they were naked

because the naked body symbolizes our brute objectivity. Putting on clothing signifies laying claim to the right of being the subject, of seeing without being seen.

I "am" my possibilities, and the order of the instruments that are in the world "is the image of my possibilities,"[12] that is, the image of what I am. Through action I unknowingly adapt myself to this image. The Other, whom I have made an object (in my judgment, etc.) is an instrument defined for me through its relations to all other instruments. I also apprehend the Other in terms of his organization of the world around him (since he in turn makes the world a totality of *his* instruments), but the whole remains my microcosmos. Nothing is irretrievably lost. On the contrary the world reveals to me the Other together with his situation, that is, as a unity which extends throughout "the whole world as a mundane power for the synthetic organization of this world."[13]

But I structure in a wholly different manner the world in which I make the Other an object. I can never apprehend a situation as it appears to the other, and I can always be mistaken concerning the Other's intentions. It would be different if I could apprehend and communicate with the Other as subject. But that is impossible. As soon as I turn toward him, I make him and his world into objects of my world.

The for-itself, which constitutes the essence of man, is the nihilation of the in-itself; it is a degraded thing bereft of being-in-itself. Through nihilation it did indeed achieve consciousness, but it had at the same time to take upon itself the burden of facticity—a body, the quality of a "given" with respect to others, a preterite which defined it. It seeks henceforth to escape its factual existence, that is, "its being-there as an in-itself for which there is no foundation."[14] Always pursued, it flees toward an impossible future where the for-itself would be in-itself-for-itself—an in-itself with its own foundation (and not something for an outside observer). It nihilates and flees from the in-itself which is at the same time pursuing it. The for-itself is a pursued-pursuing. It is both flight and pursuit and can not be distinguished from its two-directional movement.

The continuous flight which constitutes the being of man comes to a sudden stop when the Other emerges, for the Other sees it and changes it thereby into an object, an in-itself. The reason is that for the Other I am unalterably what I actually am, and even my freedom becomes a mere quality of my being, a given; it ceases to be something experienced. I experience my objectivity as an alienation of myself, and it confers on my flight the character of the in-itself before which it flees. The in-itself recaptures me.

"Such is the origin of my concrete relations with the Other; they are wholly governed by my attitudes with respect to the object which I am for the Other."[15] The Other can look on me and know what I am; I can not know what I am, however, for I can not conceive of myself as an object. "Thus the profound meaning of my being is outside of me."[16] Since it is the Other's freedom that I have sought to make the foundation on my being-in-itself, I try to appropriate for myself this freedom, yet in such a way that it will remain an active freedom experienced and manifested by the Other. That would happen if I could incorporate his freedom. Then I would become *for myself* my own foundation, and would attain the goal of my pursuing flight. My being consists therefore in the continuously repeated attempt to make the Other an object (in order to my own foundation). "These two attempts which I am are opposed to one another."[17] If one succeeds, the other fails; the failure of either motivates the adoption of the other. These two attempts, always simultaneously undertaken, are the basis for my behavior with respect to the Other.

My relations to the Other are interchangeable. "While I attempt to free myself from the hold of the Other (who wishes to make me his object), the Other is trying to free himself

20

from mine; while I seek to enslave the Other, the Other seeks to enslave me."[18] The original meaning of being-for-others (my being-for-others and the being-for-others or being-for-me of the Other) is this conflict, not Heidegger's *Mit-sein* ("being with").

Being-for-itself is synonymous with the nihilation of the in-itself which it actually is, and with inner negation of the in-itself which is not. It transcends the world and causes there to be things. Man's being has the dual characteristic of being facticity and transcendence.

"The Other by rising up confers on the for-itself a being-in-itself-in-the-midst-of-the-world as a thing among things. This petrification in in-itself by the Other's look is the profound meaning of the myth of Medusa."[19] Of course the in-itself to which the for-itself changes under the Other's look is but the outside of the for-itself. For myself I am always a person completely different from the one that I am for the Other. "The for-itself by nature is the being which can not coincide with its being-in-itself."[20]

In several respects the human reality has to be its own nothingness. "First by temporalizing itself—i.e., by always being at a distance from itself, which means that it can never let itself be determined by its past to perform this or that particular act; second, by rising up as consciousness of something and (of) itself—i.e., by being presence to itself and not simply self, which implies that nothing exists in consciousness which is not consciousness of existing and that consequently nothing external to consciousness can motivate it; and finally, by being transcendence—i.e., not something which would *first* be in order subsequently to put itself into relation with this or that end, but on the contrary a being which is originally a project—i.e., which is defined by its end."[21]

The world, because of its very articulation, "necessarily appears to us as we are. In fact, it is by surpassing the world toward ourselves that we make it appear as it is. We choose the world, not in its contexture as in-itself but in its meaning, by choosing ourselves."[22] By denying that we are the world (internal negation of the world) we allow it to appear as world.

For human reality being is reduced to acting. Being human is an articulated unity of actions. Acting is not a *consequence* of anything at all in the world or in man; it is rather the *expression* of freedom; it is independent.

Every act is an expression of our freedom to the extent that it manifests itself as effluence of the original choice which we ourselves are; the act therefore can not be done or compensated for by another even though the original choice can be changed or is changed. That a change is always possible is attested by anguish. For in anguish we are distressed when confronted by ourselves as by one who can at any time change, on whom we can not rely for the very reason that he is free.

Because the choice by which I have chosen myself is constantly being threatened and the possibilities unfolded by it eaten away by my freedom, I must constantly reassume it. When the new choice is made, "consciousness posits its own past as an object; that is, it *evaluates* its past and takes its bearings in relation to it [though it is not determined by the past]. This act of objectivizing the immediate past is the same as the new choice of other ends."[23]

Was it possible for Adam to take the apple? Yes, but only if he changed his original choice and became a different Adam. But along with this new Adam would also have emerged a new world, and whether or not Eve would have been a part of it is unknown. The Biblical Adam could not choose to be himself (he received his being from God) and bore no responsibility for his being, that is, for his commissions and omissions.

Intention is the fundamental structure of human reality and this means that we must go beyond the given toward a result to be achieved. For this reason it can never be explained by a given (whether physical, mental, or spiritual). Nor is the end given; rather "the intention makes itself be by choosing the end which makes it known."[24] The intentional choice of the end reveals the world, not as it is but as it ought to be. The intention is nonthetic consciousness of possibilities and therefore thetic consciousness of the end. The given is judged in terms of the end: "It is in the light of non-being [the end is still nonexistent for it lies in the future, and only that which is present can be] that being-in-itself is illuminated."[25]

"To be free to-be-free-to-do."[26] This assumes that there is something independent of my existence and action. My action can reveal to me this something but is not dependent on it. "To do is precisely to change what has no need of something other than itself in order to exist; it is to act on that which on principle is indifferent to action, that which can pursue its existence or its becoming without the action."[27]

Human reality, since it is action, "can be conceived only as being at its core a rupture with the given. It is the being which *causes there to be a given* by breaking with it and illuminating it in the light of the not-yet-existing,"[28] that is, the end.

The for-itself is free and "can cause there to be a world because . . . (it) is the being which has to be what it was in the light of what it will be,"[29] that is, what it has been, in keeping with the Hegelian formula, "Essence is what has been."

"Man encounters an obstacle only within the field of his freedom. . . . There is no obstacle in an absolute sense, but the obstacle reveals its coefficient of adversity across freely invented and freely acquired techniques. The obstacle reveals this coefficient also in terms of the value of the end posited by freedom."[30]

Man can project his future but can not choose his past. "The past is that which is out of reach and which haunts us at a distance."[31]

We must make each new decision in terms of the past even though no decision is determined by the past. "The past is present and melts insensibly into the present . . . all that I am I have to be in the mode of having been . . . . Thus the importance of the past can not be exaggerated since for me '*Wesen ist was gewesen ist*,' essence is what has been."[32]

Against this, the past is only what is in relation to the end freely chosen through freedom, for it is from this end that it derives its meaning and consequently its importance. "By projecting myself toward my ends, I preserve the past with me, and by action I decide its meaning."[33] The future "decides whether the past is living or dead."[34] Once I decide through my action that the past has meaning for me, it becomes an integrating component and a necessary condition of my decision. Thus I "will" my past, and willing it means realizing it "by a thousand secondary behaviors."[35] If I decide the opposite, then the past exists only as "*that self which I no longer am—i.e.*, that being which I have *to be as the self which I am no longer.*"[36]

The extreme possibility toward which the for-itself can be projected is that of *seeing oneself*, that is, of becoming someone else in order to be able to see oneself from the outside (the magical attraction of the looking-glass).

Man is condemned to be free and therefore to bear the weight of the whole world on his shoulders. The for-itself is the prime mover of the world and itself, and therefore must wholly assume the situation together with "its peculiar coefficient of adversity, even though it be insupportable. . . . The very worst disadvantages or the worst threats which can endanger my person have meaning only in and through my project. . . . It is therefore senseless to think of complaining since nothing foreign has decided what we feel, what we live, or what we are. . . . What happens to me happens through me, and I can neither affect myself with it nor revolt against it nor resign myself to it."[37] I am always the focal point of everything that happens to me.

In anguish in the face of his freedom, man is nothing other

than a freedom "which perfectly reveals itself and whose being resides in this very revelation."[38] The one who in anguish realizes his condition "has no longer either remorse or regret or excuse."[39]

Man is the pursuit of being; the real goal of his pursuit is a "synthetic fusion of the in-itself with the for-itself."[40] Those who know the real goal of their pursuit "refrain from appropriating things for their own sake and try to realize the symbolic appropriation of their being-in-itself."[41]

Human freedom, which man becomes conscious of in anguish, is the sole source of value, for it reveals the nothingness through which the world exists. "As soon as freedom discovers the quest for being and the appropriation of the in-itself as its *own possibles*, it will apprehend by and in anguish that they are possibles only on the ground of the possibility of the other possibles."[42] But choice with respect to these possibles is guided by the value conferred on them by freedom or by the ideal presence of the *ens causa sui* or ultimate Being —the final even though unattainable human goal.

CONSCIOUSNESS

"All consciousness is positional in that it transcends itself in order to reach an object."[1] By this means it establishes the fact that the object is present. The act of establishing the presence of the object is called *positing*. Consciousness creates itself by positing.

Consciousness is "the dimension of transphenomenal being

25

in the subject."[2] It is therefore a phenomenon that transcends ordinary phenomena. It has no "'content"; it owes its being rather to positings, to the ordination of a transcendent object, that is, an object that can be reached only if the consciousness transcends itself. A table is not "in" consciousness, not even in the guise of a representation.

All man's rational and imaginative faculties are directed toward the outside (they transcend themselves); they aim at the present situation and are absorbed in it. The necessary and sufficient condition for such a positing is that the knowing consciousness be consciousness of itself as knowledge of that consciousness. Consciousness must be known to itself—it must, for example, be consciousness of being consciousness of a table—or else it would be an unconscious consciousness, and that would be absurd. Consciousness of being consciousness of this table makes it possible to state that this table exists, at least "for me." Whether it exists "in-itself" is still a moot point.

A positional consciousness of an object is at the same time a nonpositional self-consciousness—nonpositional because being consciousness of self requires the positing of no transcendental object. The nonpositional self-consciousness is correlated with the positional self-consciousness.

But there is also a reflective consciousness that posits as its object the reflected-on consciousness: "In the act of reflecting I pass judgment on the consciousness reflected-on."[3] I may be proud, for example, or dissatisfied.

The positional consciousness, in contrast, is incapable of judging itself precisely because it is directed in its entirety toward the outside. Only the reflective consciousness "turned back on itself" has this capability. But the nonreflective consciousness is of course primary and makes possible the reflective consciousness. There is a prereflective "cogito" which is the hypothesis of the cogito in the Cartesian sense.

Every conscious *Dasein* exists as consciousness of existence.

The first consciousness of consciousness is nonpositional and forms a unity with the consciousness of which it is conscious: it determines itself simultaneously as consciousness of perception and a perception. Pleasure, for example, "can not be distinguished—even logically—from consciousness of pleasure."[4] Consciousness of pleasure constitutes but does not define pleasure. "Pleasure can not exist 'before' consciousness of pleasure—not even in the form of potentiality,"[5] for such a potentiality could exist only as consciousness of being a potentiality. There is no consciousness which first is there and subsequently receives "the quality of 'conscious' like a pencil of light rays."[6] There is rather something indivisible and indissoluble, a being which is existence through and through.

"Consciousness is a plenum of existence."[7] *"Nothing* is the cause of consciousness. Consciousness is the cause of its own way of being."[8]

"Since consciousness is not *possible* before being, but since its being is the source and condition of all possibility, its existence implies its essence."[9]

Consciousness is the being of the knowing subject and is absolute. It is not relative to the experience but *is* this experience. It contains nothing substantial; it is rather pure appearance and exists only to the extent that it appears. It is absolute for the very reason that within it appearance and existence are identical. All appearances appear to consciousness. It is pure subjectivity; it is the immanence of the self.

For consciousness there is no law. "It is precisely because it is pure spontaneity, because nothing can get a grip on it that consciousness can not act upon anything."[10]

Consciousness is obliged to be intuitive knowledge of something. In this obligation lies its being, which is transcendent being that constantly oversteps itself. "For consciousness there is no being except for this precise obligation to be revealing intuition of something."[11] "Consciousness is a being such that in its being, its being is in question in so far as this being implies

27

a being other than itself."[12] This other being is the trans-phenomenal being of phenomena.

"The consciousness of man *in action* is nonreflective consciousness. It is consciousness *of something*, and the transcendent which discloses itself to this consciousness is of a particular nature; it is a *structure of exigency* in the world, and the world correlatively discloses in it complex relations of instrumentality."[13]

Consciousness "*is* because it makes itself." It "has to be its own being, it is never sustained by being; it sustains being in the heart of subjectivity, which means once more that it is inhabited by being but that it is not being: *Consciousness is not what it is*."[14] Moreover, it is consciousness of the nothingness of its being.

The unreflective consciousness is not inhabited by the ego but is consciousness of the world in general. To the extent that the self is represented in the unreflective consciousness, it is represented as *an object for the Other*. It is present to me as the self which I am and which I unwillingly experience. Only the Other knows it and he knows it not as it is for me but as it is for him.

Consciousness though unable to exist without it, is not conditioned by the given. It is "a pure and simple negation of the given, and it exists as the disengagement from a certain existing given and as an engagement toward a certain not yet existing end."[15] Moreover, it is its own negation, for it is perpetually withdrawing from itself. If it were not, it would be a pure and simple given and would have no connection with any other given.

Consciousness is an appeal to being, specifically, to the being-in-itself of things which is the object of consciousness. It is an appeal to being because it is pure subjectivity and possesses no sufficiency of being (sufficient for being). Consciousness which is conscious of itself is *other* than being. "Otherness is, in fact, an internal negation, and only a consciousness can be constituted as an internal negation."[16]

The being of self-consciousness "is the radical exclusion of all objectivity."[17] The reason is that "objectivity demands an explicit negation: the object is what I make myself not-be whereas I myself am what I make myself be. . . . Even if I could attempt to make myself an object, I would already be myself at the heart of that object which I am."[18]

FREEDOM

Man is the being who can secrete a nothingness and thereby isolate himself from other beings and things and be able to question being, that is, to subject it to interrogation. Thereby the questioned being is taken out of the series of being and freed from its causal context. At the same time the connection between the being and the questioned being is nihilated; the questioned being flees from the influence of being. This possibility of man we call freedom.

Human freedom is not a part of human existence; it precedes human existence and makes it possible. The freedom of man can not be separated from the being of man. It is the being of man's consciousness. It is not a human attribute but it is the raw material of my being. I owe my being to freedom.

Conscious being must constitute itself as being separated from its own past. "Freedom is the human being putting his past out of play by secreting his own nothingness."[1]

Human freedom is characterized by the presence (*Dasein*)

of a nothingness which interposes itself between motive and act and thereby breaks the causal connection between them. A motive exists not *in* but *for* a consciousness; it is established by consciousness. It is transcendence in immanence, and consciousness generates the nothingness which creates the motive for something transcendent.

Consciousness of freedom means consciousness of the origin of our own possibilities. In positing my own possibilities, I am positing all possibilities which have the possibility of becoming my possibilities. I call them possibilities and "sustained being."

Freedom is the basis for all human activity. "To act is to modify the shape of the world."[2] Human activity is basically intentional, goal-directed. The action necessarily implies that something will be created which has not previously existed; it implies a lack or a negativity, something not yet realized. Consciousness must therefore have the possibility of withdrawing from the world experienced in its plenitude of being (a world of which it is conscious) and of turning toward non-being; it must be able to negate its content or its self (for it is under all circumstances identical to its content). Even the most wretched situation in which a man has to live can be apprehended as defect-ridden and unbearable only when the man can conceive of another, better one. If he fails to do this, he will be unable to act to better his situation since the motive for his acts, even his existing and recognized penury, is missing. The better situation, representing the end to be attained and illuminating the defects of the present situation, is an "ideal nothingness." One who is unable to conceive of the existence of something else does not act. "For an act is a projection of the for-itself toward what is not [but what might one day be, as in the case of happiness]. And what is can in no way determine by itself what is not."[3] Since the essence of man depends on what he has been, and since man is therefore his own past, it follows that the past by itself can never give rise to an act. On the contrary, man must tear himself loose from the past (that is, from his essence and from his self) and be able to consider it in the light of a non-being if he is to make it illuminate the motive for action. The possibility of effecting a rupture with one's self is freedom.

There is no action without a cause. An action without a cause would lack an intentional structure. It would be not an action but a reaction. A phenomenon becomes a cause only if the for-itself confers on it the *value* of a cause, that is if the for-itself considers it from the viewpoint of the (still) non-existent goal. And only freedom serves this function.

I can understand my past and my present only as they relate to my future (which confers meaning on my past and present actions); in the same way the ensemble of my projects (that is, my future) confers on the cause its structure as a motive. We convert a situation into a cause or motive by fleeing from it toward the possibilities of changing it (and this again implies the possibility of achieving separation from being).

There can be no act without a cause, but this does not mean that the motive is the cause of the act. It is rather an integrating component: motive, act and goal constitute a unity which appears as a single upsurge; this upsurge is one with freedom. "Freedom makes itself an act, and we ordinarily attain it across the act which it organizes with the causes, motives, and ends which the act implies."[4]

"Freedom has no essence. It is not subject to any logical necessity."[5] Since it has no essence, I can not describe a freedom common to me and to the Other. If I wish to speak of freedom, I must speak only of my own.

Freedom, though it has no essence, is the foundation of all essentiality. For since man by virtue of the fact that he "is" constantly transcends the world in the direction of his possibilities (which he "is"), he constantly reveals the essentiality of the world that he has transcended.

31

Freedom is a contingent existent, a purely factual (and not a logical) necessity from which I receive definite information. I apprehend my freedom through my acts.

"For the for-itself, to be is to nihilate the in-itself which it is. Under these conditions freedom can be nothing other than this nihilation. It is through this that the for-itself escapes its being as its essence; it is through this that the for-itself is always something other than what can be said of it."[6] In the last analysis, the for-itself eludes denomination, for when we have said the final word about it, it is no longer what it was when we began our discourse. Man is free. I am beyond the reach of myself and others, but by this very fact I am "condemned to exist forever beyond my essence, beyond the causes and motives of my act. I am condemned to be free."[7]

Man is free but lacks the freedom not to be free. The great respect accorded causal law is attributable to the possibility of using it to conceal freedom. I will not admit that I am completely free and that motives are what I make them. The for-itself tries at the very least to have the being-in-itself of a thing and to confer permanence on causes and motives. Similarly, I wish that the end of my acts were not posited by me but that I might encounter them in the world at the time of my upsurge. I want them to originate from God, from nature, from "my" nature, from society. "These ends ready made and pre-human will therefore define the meaning of my act even before I conceive it, just as causes as pure psychic givens will produce it without my even being aware of them."[8] All these attempts to stifle my freedom are vain and collapse with the sudden upsurge of anguish in the face of freedom and the stark recognition of the reality of freedom.

An existent which is exactly what it is and which therefore is pure positivity can not be free. Freedom exists only as a potential gamut ranging from negative to positive. "Freedom is precisely the nothingness which is *made-to-be* at the heart of man and which forces human reality *to make itself* instead of *to be*.[9] (Hence the expression, "It is still not right but will soon right itself.") If man were already a plenum, then it would be absurd to look for spheres in which he would be free. "As well look for emptiness in a container which one has filled beforehand up to the brim."[10]

Freedom forms a unity with the being of the for-itself, and man is free in direct proportion to the extent to which he has to be his own nothingness.

A free being is one who makes decisions relating to his past in the light of his future and who does not let himself be determined by the present. He makes his essence known by his end (toward which he projects himself from the other side of the world which he transcends).

Even the most trivial action is not simply the consequence of the prior psychic state; on the contrary, it is an accessory component in the overall structure of my primary project, and in the totality of what I am. My primary project concerns my total being-in-the-world; its end is "a certain type of relation to being which the for-itself wills to adopt."[11]

Every act is a comprehensible phenomenon to the extent that it is "a turning back of the future toward the present."[12] It is comprehensible as a project of the itself in the direction of a possible.

The fundamental act of freedom is "a choice of myself in the world" and at the same time "a discovery of the world."[13] This choice can not be deliberate since it is the foundation of all deliberation and since "deliberation requires an interpretation in terms of an original choice."[14] The choice is not unconscious, however, for it "is simply one with the consciousness which we have of ourselves."[15] To will to love and to love are one, for "to love is to choose oneself as loving by assuming consciousness of loving."[16]

Because we project ourselves, we "are" the solution of the problem of being. By setting ourselves up as a problem, we allow the solution to exist and by experiencing it we grasp it.

The project of my self is contingent and without justification. I am always in a positon to consider this project objectively and "to make-it-past by causing the liberating *instant* to arise."[17] This instant marks the beginning of a new project and the end of the old one—in a sense, my becoming a new man. Such extraordinary instants "have often appeared to furnish the clearest and most moving image of our freedom."[18]

Freedom "is a *choice* of its being but not the foundation of its being. . . . This choice is absurd, not because it is without reason but because there has never been any possibility of not choosing oneself. . . . It is absurd in this sense—that the choice is that by which all foundation and all reasons come into being, that by which the very notion of the absurd receives its meaning."[19]

The coefficient of adversity in things—incontestably at hand —is no argument against freedom since it arises only when we posit an end. If we will nothing, nothing offers us resistance. Though from the start brute things can "limit our freedom of action, it is our freedom itself which must first constitute the framework, the technique, and the ends in relation to which they will manifest themselves as limits."[20]

A mountain peak reveals itself as insurmountable only becauses we have previously considered it as surmountable. Our freedom "constitutes the limits which it will subsequently encounter."[21]

"We are free when the final term by which we make known to ourselves what we are is an end; that is, not a real existent which could fulfill our wish, but an object which does not yet exist."[22]

Freedom is separated from (a necessary condition if the end is transcendent) and rejoined to its end by existents that offer resistance; it orders these existents and uses them to pursue its end. "There can be a free for-itself only as engaged in a resisting world."[23]

34

What freedom projects is, generally speaking, "to *do* in a resisting world by means of a victory over the world's resistances."[24] Freedom is constituted in terms of the independence of things, and in every project there implicity resides a certain margin of unpredictability (in their temples the Romans reserved a place for the unknown god). When something unforeseeable actually happens, therefore, we are not surprised but simply say, "This was bound to happen."

To be free means not to attain what has been willed, but to choose through oneself to will. The failure of a projected action does not concern freedom itself. Freedom is not the possibility of attaining chosen goals but is the autonomy of the act of choosing. A prisoner does not have the freedom to leave his prison but he has the freedom to choose to attempt to escape (instead of desisting from any attempt to escape). He can therefore project his escape and immediately convince himself—since the choice can not be separated from the act—of the value of his project. His escape is either a success or a failure.

Just as speech expresses thought and just as our words can inform us of our thoughts; so our acts inform us of our intentions.

The for-itself, though free, is not its own foundation, for if it were, then freedom (which the for-itself is) would have to choose the existence of its being. But it can not be choice of itself as freedom. We are condemned to be free. "If, therefore, freedom is defined as the escape from the given, from fact, then there is a fact of escape from fact. This is the facticity of freedom. . . . It is not master of the fact that *there is* a freedom which makes known to itself what it is by means of its end."[25] "The fact of not being able not to be free is the facticity of freedom and the fact of not being able not to exist is its *contingency*. Contingency and facticity are really one; there is a being which freedom has to be in form of *nonbeing* (that is, of nihilation)."[26]

Freedom is not simple potency but is determined by its very upsurge as a "doing," and therefore as the nihilation of something given. "One does something *with* or *to* something."[27] Freedom is the nihilation of a being which it *is* (one does not escape from a prison unless imprisoned) and in the midst of which it is.

In relation to a particular state of things I am free when it does not constrain me.

Freedom is internality and the inner negation of the given. By making itself a choice, it denies its contingency. By illuminating the plenitude of being of a being which does not yet exist (the end), freedom colors it with insufficiency and negativity. The given is freedom itself insofar as it exists and can not escape its existence, for we know that the given is "the in-itself nihilated by the for-itself which has to be it, that the body as point of view on the world, that the past as the *essence* which the for-itself was—that these are three designations for a single reality."[28]

"The true limit of my freedom lies purely and simply in the very fact that an Other apprehends me as the Other-as-object and in that second corollary fact that my situation ceases for the Other to be a situation and becomes an objective form in which I exist as an objective structure."[29]

"Freedom is total and infinite, which does not mean that it *has* no limits but that it *never encounters them*."[30]

THE OTHER AND HIS LOOK*

In shame the phenomenon of the Other confronts me. I am ashamed when the Other sees me make an awkward or vulgar gesture. Then I appear to the Other not as a subject but as an object. This makes it possible for me to pass judgment on myself as on an object—objectively. In shame "I recognize that I *am* as the Other sees me."[1] The Other sees me in a way that I can not see myself. This means that the Other establishes in me a new type of being capable of supporting qualities which I did not previously possess. "This being was not in me potentially before the appearance of the Other, for it could not have found any place in the For-itself."[2] It could not have manifested itself in me as I was before.

The appearance of the Other is manifested to me in the first place as a series of optical phenomena (gestures of every type, actions, patterns of behavior, and the like) which relates to an organizing unity. This unity is the "person" of the Other; in principle it is located beyond the reach of my experience. In the sphere of my experience there emerges a connected group of phenomena which is constituted "by a being who is not *me*."[3] These phenomena, in contrast to all other phenomena, relate not to experiences which belong to my own possibilities (and consequently to experiences which are possibles for me) but to experiences which belong to a system

---

* French requires the masculine pronoun in the case of *autrui* "other." Tr.

inaccessible to me (and which have as their center the Other). In the same way there are in my experience events which relate to the Other as a connected system of representations which are not mine. Nor is the other simply present to unify the phenomena through which I experience his presence; certain categories of phenomena seem rather to exist only for him. "The Other is not only the one whom I see but the one *who sees me*."[4] For this reason I can determine as object the Other who denies my character as subject and determines me as his object.

Heidegger affirms the existence of an ontological and therefore an *a priori* "being-with" Others. If there were such a "being-with," however, "all ontic connection with a concrete human-reality which would arise *for-itself* as an absolute transcendent"[5] would be rendered impossible.

If the Other were nothing other than an object, his existence would be purely probable (the same holds for the existence of every object which is not necessary but only probable) and would be valid or subject to validation. But this existence requires no validation; he is there just as I myself am there, and accordingly is no object among other objects. What I perceive of the Other relates not to a separate existence but to my "being-in-a-pair-with-the-Other." "My relation to the Other is first and fundamentally a relation of being to being, not of knowledge to knowledge."[6] In this original relation the Other is not first given to me as object and later revealed in a round-about way as subject; on the contrary, he is given to me directly as subject, not in the same way that I am subject for myself, but as a transcendence like the one I myself am, with the particular distinction of being a "transcended transcendence." This indicates that the other is capable of transcending the things that he encounters (that is, going beyond his own possibilities), but is at the same time transcended by me (by the very fact that I observe him and make him into an "object"). This fundamental relation is "the very type of my being-for-others."[7]

When a man comes into my fields of vision as a man rather than as an object, the distance between him and the other objects changes. Formerly the distance from object A to object B was identical to the distance from B to A and therefore reversible, but now distances unfold themselves *starting* from the man and *extending* to the objects. There is now a univocal spatial relation, without parts and given simultaneously, "inside of which there unfolds a spatiality which is not *my* spatiality; for instead of a *grouping toward me* of the objects, there is now an orientation *which flees from me*."[8] This relation without parts and without distance I express by saying, for example, "this man sees that object." When a man appears in my universe there appears among its objects an element of disintegration. A total space "is grouped around the Other, and this space is made with *my* space."[9] Within this new room things turn toward the Other face which I can not see (I do not see *how* brightly the sun shines for other men); qualities change and I can know nothing about them. "Everything is in place; everything still exists for me; but everything is traversed by an invisible flight and fixed in the direction of the new object"[10] (for the Other is still an object for me). The Other robs me of my world.

Since it is through me that a world exists, I can not be an object for myself. Nor can I be an object for the Other as long as he is an object. "A radical conversion of the Other is necessary if he is to escape objectivity."[11] This conversion takes place when the other sees me. This "being-seen-by-the-Other" is an irreducible fact. It is the truth of my "seeing-the-Other." The Other is the one who is looking at me.

The look which I apprehend on being seen relates as a rule to two eyes focused on me, but it may also be revealed by the rustling of twigs behind the bench on which I am sitting or by the sound of footsteps. Even the windows of a house have the function of a look if I happen to be about to break into the house; it is even possible for me to apprehend the windows as a look. "What I apprehend immediately when I hear the branches crackling behind me is not that *there is someone there*; it is that I am vulnerable, that I have a body which can be hurt, that I occupy a place and that I can not in any case escape from the space in which I am without defense—in short, *that I am seen*."[12]

The Other is free, exactly as I am free. His "freedom is revealed to me across the uneasy indetermination of the being which I am for him"[13] when he looks at me (I can not know, of course, what I am for him). But I am this being "objectively" and as a certainty (my shame is my proof), and I then find myself in a situation "where the very stuff of my being is the unpredictable freedom of another."[14]

By virtue of the very fact that the Other exists, my transcendence is closed in and acquires an outside; even though it escapes me and is unknowable as such, I acquire a nature. "My original fall is the existence of the Other."[15]

I "am" always my nonthetic consciousnes of my own possibilities, but the Other's look alienates them from me and at the same time alienates me from myself. Previously I was able to grasp thetically these possibilities which I have in relation to the world and in the world. When I am seen, I am seen as an object in a world that is not my world and in which everything is ordered from the viewpoint of the Other. As an object in an alien world I myself am alienated and the world which I have organized becomes alien to me. I become "somebody." My possibilities are surpassed by the Other toward his own possibilities. The other as a look is—my transcendence transcended. My possibilities, once they are surpassed by the other, become dead possibilities: they become inert; they lie beyond me; I can view them from without ("through the Other's eyes") and see their worth. All this can happen because I know intuitively that "the Other is the hidden death of my possibilities insofar as I live that death as hidden in the midst of the world."[16]

Since the possibilities alienated from me by the Other lie beyond me (they are no longer *my* possibilities), they take on an objective character and become mere probabilities. The result is that I am no longer master of the situation. There emerges, along with the upsurge of the Other, something unpredictable, an aspect of the situation which is for the Other and not for me. This is "the unpredictable but still real *reverse side*"[17] of the situation. This limited translucency of the situation, the distinguishing mark of our being-in-the-midst-of-the-world-for-others, has been by Kafka in *The Trial*; and here God replaces the Other.

The Other's look causes me to experience simultaneity. The world does not comprehend simultaneity, for all beings are linked together by my single presence in this world. Simultaneity exists only between two distinct systems. "It supposes the co-presence to the world of two presences considered as presences-to."[18] A certain glass, for example, exists for me at the same time that it exists for the Other.

"To be looked at is to apprehend oneself as the unknown object of unknowable appraisals"[19] on the part of the Other. At the same time, however, I apprehend the appraisals as "a free surpassing of the given toward possibilities. A judgment is the transcendental act of a free being. Thus being-seen constitutes me as a defenseless being or a freedom which is not my freedom."[20] I become a slave in the Hegelian sense. "I am a slave to the degree that my being is dependent at the center of a freedom which is not mine and which is the very condition of my being,"[21] namely my being-for-others which is as much part and parcel of me as is my being-for-itself. At the same time, however, I am constantly in danger of being transformed by the Other into an instrument which may be used as means to ends of which I am ignorant.

The Other is the one who looks at me and the being at whom

I am not looking. As soon as I look at him, he becomes a part of the world and loses the structure that characterizes him as the Other. "In the phenomenon of the look, the Other is on principle that which can not be object."[22] The Other is boundless, endless, incomprehensible subjectivity. He is in addition unbounded freedom.

The presence of the Other is "the supporting environment of my being-unrevealed,"[23] for as noted earlier, it produces in me new, previously unknown qualities. The Other can not be distinguished from the alienation of my possibilities and the flow of my world toward another world, for he is their meaning and direction. That which the Other is, is never more present and more urgent than when I am unaware of it.

I can never be an object for myself. As soon as I start to reflect on myself, I tacitly assume the Other's existence, for I act "as if" I were an object for myself or—something that amounts to the same thing—"as if" I were an Other for myself. The Other makes it possible for me to seize upon my objectivity (which is contained in my subjectivity or person). "If I am able to conceive of even one of my properties in the objective mode, then the Other is already given."[24]

I do not recognize myself-as-object, and yet through the Other "I know that 'it is me.' "[25] It is the fact of the presence of the Other, made known to me through uneasiness. This uneasiness reveals to me inescapable being-for-others. Through the Other's upsurge, I am separated and alienated from myself. The Other's presence is scandalous.

When we have to come forward openly, say, to act in a play or to give a lecture, we do not apprehend a "plural" look with respect to the audience that sees us. "It is a matter rather of an intangible reality, fleeting and omnipresent, which realizes the unrevealed Me confronting us and which collaborates with us in the production of this Me which escapes us."[26] As soon as I look attentively at the audience to make certain that they are following my thought, however, this reality is objectivized and decomposed into a plurality of heads and eyes. It is with respect to the prenumerical *concrete* reality that we may properly use the term "they." "Wherever I am, *they* are perpetually looking at me."[27] With every attempt to apprehend it as object, "they" disintegrates.

To the extent that I cause there to be a world and along with it the Other, I am also the cause of his subjectivity and his knowledge of me. As long as the Other remains my object, his subjectivity is merely the ensemble of his objective qualities, though not of his subjective qualities which he uses to his own advantage. And since an Object can not make me into an Object, I remain myself, and the knowledge which the Other has of me can not endanger me, does not affect me; it is simply an image of me in him, one that may be true or false but that in no way concerns me. Through my upsurge in the world I cause the Other to be an object among objects in the midst of the world, I cause the world to shape itself around him; that is, I cause him to be "in situation" and to create for me the objective unity which I need to organize things as instruments or obstacles in the-world. For the Other can at any time reverse the situation by looking at me; he then becomes subject and makes me an object. The Other-as-object is "an explosive instrument which I handle with care."[28] I therefore take pains to contain the Other in his objectivity and to remain his master. But I enjoy only temporary success, and only the dead are perpetually objects incapable of ever becoming subjects.

It may be that I choose at the moment of my upsurge into the world to look at the look of the Other (whereupon the look and its objectifying power disappear, leaving only the eyes) and to build my subjectivity on the collapse of the Other's freedom (that is, therefore, on the Other-as-object). This attitude we call indifference toward others. I become blind to the Other's transcendence. For me the Other is only a magic object that can act at a distance and that I can act upon under certain circumstances. "I brush against 'people' as I brush against a wall; I

43

avoid them as I avoid obstacles. Their freedom-as-object is for me only their 'coefficient of adversity.'[29] What they know about me does not concern me. They perform certain functions of varying usefulness. They are mechanisms which I can release if I know the key word ("Waiter! A beer, please!"). This blindness may be extended over a whole life-time. "There are men who die without—save for brief and terrifying flashes of illumination—ever having suspected what the Other is."[30] My behavior enables me to feel wholly secure. Indeed, I never experience anything more certain concerning my objectivity (which I still am *also*) and I am always alone against the terrible necessity of being free and accepting the responsibility for making-myself-be. Therefore I always have a definite comprehension of the reality of the Other's freedom. My attitude toward the Other is therefore fundamentally false. Besides, I am seen and possessed by the other; I am defenseless, for I deny the Other as freedom. I am in danger without realizing it. The result of all this is unrest and discomfort.

My actions toward the other are uncertain and inconstant. They are directed at one moment toward the Other as toward the object which I intend to use for my end and at the next toward the Other as toward the subject through whom I intend to learn who in reality, that is, "objectively," I am. "At whatever moment a person is considered, he is one or the other of these attitudes—unsatisfied by the one as by the other. We can maintain ourselves for a greater or lesser length of time in the attitude adopted depending on our bad faith or depending on the particular circumstances of our history. But never will either attitude be sufficient in itself; it always points obscurely in the direction of its opposite."[31] But there can be no attitude in which the Other will be revealed simultaneously as object and as subject, as a fixed transcendent power and as actual freedom. There is no way out. My mere upsurge in the Other's world sets an objective limit on the Other's freedom, and my own act is executed in a world where the Other already is and where in relation to him I am superfluous.

"Human-reality remains alone because the Other's existence has the nature of a contingent and irreducible fact. We encounter the *Other*; we do not constitute him."[32] From the outside what the Other experiences as a free project has the value of a technique or a process which can be imitated because it looks like an object to me. Yet the very fact of the Other's existence is the cause of the collective ownership of techniques through which I attempt to appropriate the world. I am cast into a world "which is revealed to me only by collective and already constituted techniques. . . . These techniques are going to determine my belonging to collectivities: to the *human race*, to the national collectivity, to the professional and to the family group."[33] Now these techniques which I have not chosen confer on the world its (objective) meaning."[34]

"To come into the world as a freedom confronting Others is to come into the world as alienable."[35] To freedom belongs the passion of freedom. Through the free assumption of my being-for-others which I experience, I also recognize the transcendence of the Other and experience my objective being. This assumption is also "made in the perspective of my fundamental project."[36] and though the meanings which I assume are indeed for the Other, they can also have meaning for me if I choose them and therefore call in my freedom. "I do not choose to be for the Other what I am, but I can try to be for myself what I am for the Other, by choosing myself as I appear to the other."[37]

WE

The expression "we" is used to designate a group of subjects to which we ourselves belong. The subjects mutually agree to leave their subjectivity intact; they do not try to change each other into objects (of judgment, etc.); among them there is no conflict. As a rule they have a common object, such as a spectacle on the theatrical stage, on the street, or in a crowd.

There is no intersubjective consciousness which could be designated as "we." It is "a certain particular experience which is produced in special cases on the foundation of being-for-others in general."[1] But there is also a "we" which is experienced and which is designated in the statement, "We are being looked at by those people."

In the role of we-as-object, we are objects among objects. "We experience it in shame as a community alienation."[2] That can happen, for instance, if I am struggling with the Other when a Third suddenly appears, makes us into objects of his judgment, alienates my possibilities and the Other's, and radically changes thereby the situation in which we found ourselves. There is in the world of the Third an objective situation "in which the Other and I figure as *equivalent* structures in *solidarity* with each other,"[3] while in my own world the Other is either superior or inferior to me (depending on whether at a given moment he is with respect to me subject or object) and I find myself constantly in conflict with him. Through the Third my relation to the Other acquires a being-outside; I am organized with the Other as a whole in which I am fundamentally no longer distinct from the Other. By experiencing my solidarity with the Other through the Third, I experience the Us-object. For the Third we are "them" and this "them" we assume as the meaning which our "we" has objectively, for the Third. At the same time we assume the totality that we constitute with the Other, and also the responsibility for the Other (because we have become solidary with him) and for the totality. Being made into an us-object is therefore a harsh, oppressive experience. "The one who experiences himself as constituting an Us with other men feels himself trapped among an infinity of strange existences; he is alienated radically and without recourse."[4]

To be sure, the Third through whom I apprehend myself as us-object can also be a collectivity, a sociological class, mankind as a whole, God. The oppressing class, for example, plays the role of the Third with respect to the oppressed class; it produces the experience of us-object and class consciousness and through its look constitutes the oppressed class.

We live in a world of manufactured objects, and each of these objects refers to subjects *for* whom it is manufactured. The worker in producing an object experiences in his work his being-an-instrument for others. Work for others is a mode of alienation. The alienating subject is the consumer, the "they" who in some way make their wishes known to the worker. These wishes constitute the end of the object and the activity of the worker. An object that I use makes me known to myself as "they." If many men use the same manufactured object (for instance, a telephone), the uses for which the object is intended of necessity bring about the experience of we-subject. "The experience of the We-subject is a pure psychological, subjective event in a single consciousness; it corresponds to inner modification of the structure of this consciousness but does not appear on the foundation of a concrete ontological relation with others and does not realize any *Mitsein*."[5] Only with the help of things in the world do I become an object of We-subject. This "we" disappears when the things that I use disappear.

Not all objects that I use for my purposes refer to a manufacturer or to an Other. For instance, in confronting a rock that I use as a hammer "I have a nonthetic consciousness of myself as a person; that is, of my selfness, of my ends, and of my free inventiveness."[6] Nor does an object appear as manufactured unless I have in some way experienced the Other's existence. If I lack this experience, I can in no way discover that the object has been manufactured by someone and look on it as a natural product of nature especially well adapted to a certain purpose. Though I may utilize it in an appropriate way, my action must be attributed in this case to my own discovery and not to the manufacturer's intention. "If therefore the manufactured object refers to others and thereby to my undifferentiated transcendence, this is because I already know others,"[7] and not because I possess *Mitsein*.

"Thus there is no symmetry between the making proof of the us-object and the experience of the we-subject. The first is the revelation of a dimension of real existence and corresponds to a simple enrichment of the original proof of the for-others. The second is a psychological experience realized by an historic man immersed in a working universe and in a society of a definite economic type. It reveals nothing particular; it is purely subjective *Erlebnis*."[8] Quite apart from the reality of the we-experience, however, there still remains the dilemma of whether to transcend or be transcended by the Other.

LANGUAGE

Language consists of patterns of experience through which I try to impose on the other my point of view, to dominate him and enslave him. The spoken language is but one subordinate form of language in general. "Language is . . . originally being-for-others; that is, it is the fact that a subjectivity experiences itself as an object for the Other."[1] In this sense I am what I say and men are what they say (Hölderlin). Language is the original proof which the for-itself can make of its being-for-others. When the Other emerges before me, language also emerges as the condition of my being.

I never know, however, what effect my language will have on the Other who hears it, for he is of course freedom and confers on my language its meaning. "I never know exactly if I signify what I wish to signify nor even if I am signifying anything."[2] Each thought that I wish to express through my language requires the help of an alien freedom in order to constitute itself as object. "Language reveals to me the freedom (the transcendence) of the one who listens to me in silence,"[3] and is therefore something sacred. For the Other, however, language is something magical, for it is an action at a distance and has for him the property of a magical object (which I am for him). The problems of language are the same as those of love.

Language is the reality of speech, dialect (or jargon) is the reality of language, and the reality of dialect is "the *free act* of designation by which I choose myself as *designating*,"[4] that

49

is, as one who wishes to designate something through the medium of expression of language. "And this free act can not be an *assembling* of words."[5] It is by speaking that we cause words to exist and thereby found the necessity of technical connectives or articulation within the sentence."[6] "It is by speaking that I make grammar,"[7] but for the listener speech has specific, fixed boundaries.

The basic unit of speech is not the word but the freely contrived sentence. I understand the meaning of a sentence only to the extent that I understand the situation in terms of which it has been formulated by the speaker. This *meaning* is "an end chosen in a free surpassing of means," that is, the linguistic apparatus; it is a *designation* of grammatical relations.

ANGUISH

In anguish I experience anguish before myself and, because my freedom makes it unpredictable and unforseeable, before my own conduct. My conduct, which expresses my possibilities, provokes anguish for the very reason that it is merely possible and does not constitute a sure basis for a definite, purposive procedure.

I am not yet the self that I will be. As soon as I begin to speak of myself, I note that something is out of order. For to speak of myself means to speak of the self that I have been until now since the self that I have been can be made the object of thinking and speaking. I am, however, no object but a subject. This means that I must continuously disengage myself or tear myself apart from the self that I am at the present instant. The result is, however, that I am *the* man whom I can describe, not for myself, but for the Other onlooker, for others. For myself I am the self that moves toward the goal that I have selected. I am suspended in midair between the self that I have been until now and the self that I will be, and this state of suspension is my present, my characteristic being; this self is always "postponed." I am incited and compelled to attain the end previously chosen. For myself I am the self that I have to be. And since I can at any time change the compelling goal—and actually am constantly changing it—I never know who I will be. It can also be said that "*I am the self which I will be in the mode of not being it.*"[1] Consciousness of this fact is anguish.

"The self which I am depends on the self which I am not yet to the exact extent that the self which I am not yet does not depend [thanks to my freedom] on the self which I am."[2] This results in anguish in the face of the future. Anguish is my consciousness of my freedom. I experience anguish in the face of the nothingness that separates the motive from the act, the past from the present. In anguish I recognize a possibility as *mine*, that is, as a possibility projected by my freedom and therefore not determining. My present is not justified by my past and my future lies beyond my reach. My freely choosen end is not binding. I am in anguish because I no longer see before me a definite instant, nor even one that lies in the near future.

"In anguish we do not simply apprehend the fact that the possibles which we project [and posit as ends] are perpetually eaten away by our freedom-to-come; in addition we apprehend our choice—*i.e.* ourselves—as *unjustifiable*. This means that we apprehend our choice as not deriving from any prior reality."[3]

To hide from ourselves our anguish, we act as if our ends were prescribed by the Other [nature, society, God]or as if our possibilities did not depend solely on our freedom but were engendered by a fixed and already constituted thing—the self which from our particular viewpoint is envisioned and described as if it were another person. "Thus we flee from anguish by attempting to apprehend ourselves from without as an Other or as a thing."[4] But we can hide from ourselves our anxiety only because and so long as we have knowledge of it. In order to take care not to think of our anxiety, we must think of it constantly. We *are* anxiety, and we must be anxiety, for otherwise we could not be conscious of our freedom and therefore of our humanity.

BAD FAITH

Bad faith is any type of lie through which I deliberately suppress from myself that truth which I know and through which to a certain degree I deceive myself. To be capable of bad faith I need the Other only when involved in a situation which can be influenced for my benefit through the help of bad faith.

I can not deliberately deceive myself, however, for I can see into the heart of my consciousness. The result is that my bad faith, as soon as it appears, begins to disappear and give way to cynicism. It is a mutable psychic structure. But it does present a durable form, and a person can spend a whole lifetime in bad faith.

Psychoanalysis holds that in bad faith my (conscious) ego is deceived by my (unconscious) id without awareness on my part. The id is in possession of a truth of which I have no knowledge and from which the id excludes me by deceiving me. I am excluded by the id's deception. This interpretation is unacceptable. The equally "unconscious" superego (moral consciousness), which in the role of censor determines what shall pass from the id to the ego and in what form passage will occur, would need to have the capacity to represent something and choose it from a host of representations. Otherwise it would be impossible to explain how the superego can sometimes discontinue its vigilance and how it can be deceived by the id. Therefore the censor must be conscious of the role which it has to play. It must be conscious of being consciousness of the drive to be repressed; yet it must not—according to the theory of psychoanalysis—be conscious of this fact, for then it would be in bad faith. But the drive must also be conscious of being represented by the censor; otherwise it could not be symbolically distinguished in such a way as to pass by the censor unrecognized. Psychoanalysis has split the natural unity of the psychic mechanism into three parts (id, ego, superego) and still has not created the possibility of clarifying the phenomenon of bad faith or of self-deception.

Facticity and transcendence are two aspects of human reality. They can and must be intellectually co-ordinated. Bad faith resorts to the artifice of affirming their identity while preserving their differences. It operates in such a way that there is a continuous shifting from one to the other. The same holds for the being-for-others of the human reality, which actually exists only as complements, that is, as mutually complementary modes of being.

Example: A woman meets a man in a cafe. She knows perfectly well what his intentions are and that he is constantly transcending (going beyond) the situation (sitting at a table, drinking coffee, smoking cigarettes, discussing the latest film) in the direction of the end that he has chosen: to possess the woman. But she acts as if this were an innocent meeting or friendly conversation with no strings attached and as if the situation itself were not "transcendent" but "factitious," that is, as if it were only what it is. At the same time the woman would be unhappy if the situation really were nothing more than it appears to be, for the charm of the situation resides for her in the fact that she finds the situation pleasurable for the very reason that she can detect in his every word and gesture the man's particular intention or "project." Thus the transcendence and the facticity of the situation blend even as their differences —that is, the false and the true meaning of the situation—are perserved. The woman finds herself in the state of bad faith and enjoys this state as an engaging sport.

In the world of bad faith there appears a "*non-persuasive evidence.*"[1] The man in bad faith is resolved in advance not to require too much by way of proof. When convenient he persuades himself to accept uncertain truths. Through bad faith he is convinced that his own "metastable" structure is the structure of the world and that "nonpersuasion is the structure of all convictions."[2]

Bad faith is possible "because consciousness conceals in its being a permanent risk of bad faith. The origin of this risk is the fact that the nature of consciousness simultaneously is to be what it is not and not to be what it is."[3]

THE LIE

The lie is a natural manifestation of what Heidegger calls *Mitsein,* that is, our original and conflicting relation with others. The liar—in contrast to the person in bad faith—is quite clear about the lie that he wishes to articulate and to pass off for something which he knows or supposes others will accept as the truth.

In the lie consciousness furnishes proof that it is hidden from the other. "It utilizes for its own profit the ontological duality of myself and myself in the eyes of the Other."[1] The Other is not and will never be what I am; he can not look "inside my heart" even if he stands as close as possible to me. Two lovers will never be joined together as one; on the contrary, each must endure deep, ontological loneliness and solitude. The Other can know what goes on in but one consciousness—his own. I can therefore deceive him and always deceive him if my project requires deception in order to illuminate and transcend the situation, for this project is the "truth" of my conduct with respect to things and to the Other.

EXISTENTIAL PSYCHOANALYSIS

Man is a personal unity of all that can be said about him. Here "personal" means that the unity which constitutes the being of the man under consideration is a *free unification*. It is absurd to try—as Freudian psychoanalysis does—to re-construct a person by positing these inclinations as irreducibles (that is, as not susceptible of being reduced to underlying causes). For example, an alleged desire "if presented as an irreducible is an absurd contingency and involves in absurdity human reality taken as a whole."[1]

Man's inclination is not something fundamental but rather something secondary and derived; it is secondary with respect to the fundamental project through which he makes himself what he is and it derives from the structure of this project.

Stendhal and Proust "have shown that love and jealousy can not be reduced to the strict desire of possessing a *particular* woman, but that these emotions aim at laying hold of the world in its entirety through the woman."[2]

In each tendency, inclination, or attitude the person expresses himself completely. Every attitude has a meaning by which it is transcended; it signifies "the total relation to the world by which the subject constitutes himself as a self."[3] It is the expression of the free choice of an intelligible character; indeed, it *is* this choice effected in relation to the given circumstances.

If concrete attitudes are the expression of the fundamental choice, then the subject's fundamental choice is the expression of nothing other than "the individual secret of the subject's being-in-the-world."[4] In the fundamental choice I choose my being; I choose to be. "The for-itself is a being such that in its being, its being is in question in the form of a project of being. To the for-itself *being* means to make known to oneself what one is by means of a possibility appearing as a value. Possibility and value belonging to the being of the for-itself: The for-itself is defined ontologically as a *lack of being,* and possibility belongs to the for-itself as that which it lacks, in the same way that value haunts the for-itself as the totality of being which is lacking. . . . The for-itself chooses because it is lack; freedom is the concrete mode of being of the lack of being."[5] It follows that the psychoanalyst has hit upon the obvious irreducible when and only when in the course of treatment he reaches the fundamental project of being. "Fundamentally man is the *desire to be,*"[6] and the original project which finds expressions in each of our empirically observed inclinations, tendencies, or attitudes is the project of being, that is, the decision to be.

The being which the for-itself lacks is the in-itself. The for-itself emerges as a nihilation of the in-itself, and this nihilation is defined as the project toward the in-itself. Between the nihilated in-itself and the projected in-itself the for-itself is nothing. "Thus the end and the goal of the nihilation which I am is the in-itself."[7] The desire for being of human reality is the desire for being-in-itself.

But the projected in-itself can not be identical to the nihilated in-itself. The projected in-itself is an in-itself nihilated in for-itself; it is accordingly an in-itself that is what the for-itself is. It is a consciousness that the for-itself "wishes to have the impermeability and infinite density of the in-itself. It is as the nihilation of the in-itself and a perpetual evasion of contingency and of facticity that it wishes to be its own foundation."[8] The for-itself wishes therefore to be in-itself and yet to avoid contingency; it wishes to be an in-itself conscious of itself. "This is why the possible is projected in general as what the for-itself lacks in order to become in-and-for-itself. The fundamental value which presides over this project is exactly the in-itself-for-itself; that is, the ideal of a consciousness which would be the foundation of its own being-in-itself by the pure consciousness which it would have of itself. It is this ideal which can be called God."[9]

"Existential psychoanalysis rejects the hypothesis of the unconscious; it makes the psychic act co-extensive with consciousness."[10] This means that the fundamental project is experienced by the subject and is wholly conscious but it certainly does not mean that the project is known by him. And what is apprehended through reflection is not the project itself but the behavior through which it finds expression. Reflection "is entirely constituted by a pre-ontological comprehension of the fundamental project,"[11] but is incapable of fixing it by concepts. "It is penetrated by a great light without being able to express what this light is illuminating."[12] Reflection "will simply furnish us with the brute materials toward which the psychoanalyst must take an objective attitude. Thus only will he be able to *know* what he already *understands*, [namely]

. . . the totality of the individual human being and the irreducible element of the transcendence with the structure of being-for-others."[13] The project-for-itself always eludes the psychoanalyst; it can be experienced only as a living possession. "There is an incompatibility between existence for-itself and objective existence."[14]

Existential psychoanalysis will not obtain as a result of its inquiry an abstract and general term such as the libido, but will consider the complex itself as the absolute choice or the choice of being which does not need to be explained through something abstract like the libido and which can not be explained. In each instance the complex proves to be irreducible.

Existential psychoanalysis abandons the notion of mechanical causation. It holds rather that the environment can influence the subject only to the extent that he understands it or makes it his situation. No objective description of the environment can yield information about the subject.

If a pattern of conduct can be considered as symbolizing the fundamental project (the complex), then a universal meaning can never be attached to the symbol. The meaning must be elaborated anew in each particular case. For the fundamental project is living, conscious choice and the subject can always change or revoke his choice.

Existential psychoanalysis is "a method destined to bring to light, in a strictly objective form, the subjective choice by which each living person makes himself a person; that is, makes known to himself what he is."[15] The behavior which it studies "will include not only dreams, failures, obsessions, and neuroses, but also and especially the thoughts of waking life, successfully adjusted acts, style, etc."[16]

LOVE

Love is one of the fundamental modes of man's being-for-others. The ideal, the end, and the worth of love consists in influencing the Other's freedom while leaving that freedom intact. In love, however—in contrast to most of my other patterns of behavior—I do not lose my objectivity and make the Other into an object. Rather I identify myself wholly with my being-looked-at "in order to maintain before me the Other's freedom which is looking at me."[1] At the same time I identify myself with the Other's freedom, for it is the foundation of my being-in-itself which I sought to found through my original project; it transcends me and makes me into a being-as-object. The ideal of being for myself an Other is the primary value of my relations to the Other.

Every attempt to join my freedom to the Other's freedom entails a conflict; love is no exception.

The lover wants to be loved by a freedom, not by a slave or an automaton; yet he longs at the same time for the freedom that loves him not to be free; he longs for it to determine itself to become love. He demands that freedom act as if it were fettered by love. And he does not want to be the cause of this radical modification of freedom but rather its "unique and privileged occasion."[2] He wants from the first to exist as the objective limit of the Other's freedom, and this is the limit which the freedom must accept to be free, that is, clearly distinguished from other modes of being. Such a limitation of freedom is in fact something given. This means that freedom will exist only within its limits and will prohibit itself from surpassing the given. The prohibition is endured by the lover as facticity and *simultaneously* sanctioned as the emanation of his own freedom. This facticity, since the lover is the factitious limit of the beloved's freedom, is in reality the lover's facticity. "Thus to want to be loved is to infect the Other with one's own facticity; it is to wish to compel him to recreate you perpetually as the condition of a freedom which submits itself and which is engaged."[3] If this end could be attained, I would no longer be insecure within the Other's consciousness, for he could no longer transcend me in the direction of his own possibilities (I am now his limit) and could therefore no longer use me as an instrument for an unknown end. I would be not only the unsurpassable, his absolute end, but the source of his value and the objective foundation of all values. If I am to be loved, I am the one through whom the world will exist for the Other. I am not someone detaching himself from the ground of the world under propitious conditions; I myself am the ground for the Other's world.

If I am to be loved, I must be freely chosen as the beloved. But the choice must not be contingent; the Other must not have chosen me because I happened in some way to meet him. Against this, I require that the free upsurge of the Other's being-in-the-world have as its sole purpose his choosing me, that he at the time of his upsurge choose himself as the one who is the foundation of my objectivity and my facticity. "I have infected him with my facticity, but as it is in the form of freedom that he has been infected with it, he refers it back to me as a facticity taken up and consented to. He is the foundation of it in order that it may be his end."[4] My facticity thereby becomes not a fact but a right. Whereas before "we felt ourselves "*de trop*" we now feel that our existence is taken up and willed even in its tiniest details by an absolute. This is the basis for the joy of love where there is joy: we feel that our existence is justified."[5]

Assimilation through love is a fusion of individual consciousnesses in which each maintains his otherness in order to found the Other. If we could interiorize and keep intact the Other's freedom, which is the foundation of our being, then we would become our own foundation; we would become in-and-for-itself.

Since the beloved is a look and can apprehend the lover as Other-as-object (like every Other), he can not enslave his own freedom; he can not will to love. The lover must seduce the beloved, and his love is indistinguishable from this seduction. "To seduce is to risk assuming my object-state completely for the Other; it is to risk the danger of *being-seen* [by desisting from looking at the other] in order to effect a new departure and to appropriate the Other in and by means of my object-ness."[6] I attempt thereby to make myself a *fascinating* object. My acts are designed to point to the unsurpassable infinity of my possibilities (transformed into dead-possibilities by the Other's look) and to the world which through my being I mediate for the Other. My acts become speech, which I direct toward the Other. I solicit his love.

But the change from being fascinated to being a lover can be effected only if the beloved projects being loved, that is, if he attempts on his part to appropriate my subjectivity as such. "In fact the only way that he could conceive to realize this appropriation is to make himself be loved. Thus it seems that to love is in essence the project [of a freedom] of making oneself beloved."[7] Love therefore embodies a contradiction. If he wishes to make himself beloved as an object (for the Other is already subject and must remain subject), the lover's freedom is alienated; it pours out into the body-for-others and "is brought into existence with a dimension of flight toward the Other."[8] Love is alienated freedom. Each lover "wants the other to love him but does not take into account the fact

61

that to love is to want to be loved and thus by wanting the other to love him, he only wants the other to want to be loved in turn."[9]

Lovers seek solitude, for when they are looked at by a third person, each lover experiences his own object-ness (with respect to the third person). The beloved becomes a transcendence-transcended for the third person and can no longer found my being. Love is fixed as a dead-possibility which is alienated from me in the direction of the third. Even if no ones sees us, we know that we exist for *all* consciousness and are being "looked at." It follows "that love as a fundamental mode of being-for-others holds in its being-for-others the seed of its own destruction."[10]

DESIRE

"My original attempt to get hold of the Other's free subjectivity through his objectivity-for-me is sexual desire."[1] It is one of our original modes of realizing our being-for-others and is in no way physiological, like hunger and thirst. Having a sex does not make man a sexual being; in contrast, however, sex is the instrument and image of his fundamental sexuality. He has a sex *because* he is for-others. "There is one mode of sexuality 'with the possibility of satisfaction,' and the developed sex represents and makes concrete this possibility."[2] But there are also other modes of sexuality.

To be sexual means to exist sexually for the Other who exists sexually for me. At the outset, whether he is of the same sex or the opposite sex is irrelevant. "It is by desiring the Other (or by discovering myself as incapable of desiring him) or by apprehending his desire for me that I discover his being-sexed. Desire reveals to me simultaneously *my* being-sexed and *his* being sexed, *my* body as sex and *his* body."[3]

The sexual act does of course free us for a short while from desire. But this liberation can not be the goal of desire, for then it would have to posit itself as an object "to be over-come"—something it can not do since it is fundamentally nonreflective. For the same reason it can posit as its goal no particular act other than ejaculation. It is in truth purely and simply desire for a transcendent object, for a human being, for a body "in a situation," that is, for a body as an organic totality. "Desire posits the world and desires the body in terms of the world. . . . Desire is nothing but one of the great forms which can be assumed by the revelation of the Other's body."[4]

Man's sexual behavior can not be traced back, therefore, to a physiological and empirical constitution. "As soon as 'there is' the body and as soon as 'there is' an *Other,* we react by desire, by *Love,* and derived attitudes."[5] Our physiological structure is only the symbolic expression of the possibility of assuming these attitudes. All other possible conducts (collaboration, conflict, rivalry, engagement, obedience, kindness, sympathy, etc.) "include as their skeleton"[6] sexual relations and are enrichments and must be interpreted as enrichments of the fundamental attitudes of love, desire, and hate. This "skeleton" is in most instances implicit, however, and "it is only seldom that one explicitly desires an Other 'of the same sex'."[7]

Desire is consciousness and a particular mode of my subjectivity. But the desiring consciousness is not one of many possible modes of consciousness. The for-itself does not choose itself as desire and thereby produce desire while remaining indifferent and unchanged; on the contrary, by choosing itself as desire the for-itself sets itself on a different plane of existence on which the relation of consciousness to its own facticity assumes a distinctive character. "The man who desires *exists* his body in a particular mode,"[8] that is, he experiences and accepts his body as a part of his facticity—the very part from which he does *not* try to flee.

Sexual desire is not only longing but also and primarily "trouble" in contrast to other forms of desire, such as hunger. Like hunger, however, it does produce a certain physical state (erection of the penis, hardening of the nipples, changes in the circulation of the blood, a rise in the temperature of the body, etc.); the desiring consciousness exists its own facticity (that is, its body together with these characteristics), and in terms of this facticity the desired body appears as desirable. But such a desire would be clear and distinct; it would not be "troubled" and would be similar to the feeling of hunger. Everyone knows "that there is a great abyss between sexual desire and other appetites."[9] Sexual desire becomes my accomplice. It falls wholly into complicity with my body. It numbs and dims consciousness. Facticity takes the initiative. "*Desire is consent to desire*"[10] and reveals to me not only the Other's body but also my own, not as a practical instrument of my conduct in the world (which it primarily is) but as pure facticity, as "a passion by which I am engaged in the world and in danger in the world."[11]

Desire for the Other's body is (at the outset) the nonthetically experienced project of being swallowed up in that very body; it is "consciousness *making itself body*."[12] In other words, "I make myself flesh *in the presence of the Other in order to appropriate* the Other's flesh."[13] While the body is always "in situation," flesh appears as pure contingency of presence. Ordinarily it is hidden, particularly by movements. "Nothing is less 'in the flesh' than a dancer even though she is nude."[14]

Desire is an attempt to cause the Other's body to exist as mere flesh. Such is the intention of caresses. They cause the

Other's body to be born as flesh to me. They are not mere strokes; when I caress the other, I cause his flesh to be born beneath my fingers. The caress divests the body of its action and cuts it off from the web of its possibilities. "*Desire is expressed by the caress as thought is by language.*"[15] The caress realizes the Other's flesh as flesh and discloses to me my own. And "I make myself flesh in order to impel the Other to realize *for-himself* and *for me* his own flesh. . . . I make her enjoy my flesh through her flesh in order to compel her to feel herself flesh."[16]

"Desire is an attitude aiming at enchantment."[17] Through the caress desire seeks to ensnare the Other's freedom in his body in such a way that the Other's whole being will come to play on the surface of his body and that by touching this body I may finally touch the Other's free subjectivity. That is why I wish to "possess" the body. Desire seeks nothing short of possession of the Other's transcendence as pure transcendence and at the same time as body. This ideal is of course unattainable.

Because movement veils flesh and makes it revert to body, caresses are effected slowly, almost imperceptibly, as if spontaneous. "It is not by chance that desire while aiming at the body as a whole attains it especially through masses of flesh which are very little differentiated, grossly nerveless, hardly capable of spontaneous movement, through breasts, buttocks, thighs, stomach: these form a sort of image of pure facticity. This is why also the true caress is the contact of two bodies in their mostly fleshly parts, the contact of stomachs and breasts; the caressing hand is too delicate, too much like a perfected instrument. But the full pressing together of the flesh of two people against one another is the true goal of desire."[18]

Desire is the affirmation of the flesh by the flesh. The submergence of consciousness in the body is accompanied by autonomous and involuntary phenomena of which the most obvious is the erection of the penis and clitoris. We can not use desire as an instrument for attaining an end. Since movements stand in opposition to the incarnation of the body, no prehensile organ can be a sex. Even in coitus the sex organs are passive: "It is the whole body which advances and withdraws, which *carries* sex forward or withdraws it. Hands help to introduce the penis; the penis itself appears as an instrument which one manages, which one makes penetrate, which one withdraws, which one utilizes. And similarly the opening and the lubrication of the vagina can not be obtained voluntarily."[19] Here as in sexual pleasure everything belongs to the realm of contingency: it happens (Latin *contigit*) that incarnation is manifested by erection and that erection ends with ejaculation. Moreover, desire itself is checked by pleasure since pleasure has as its result a reflective consciousness of desire (consciousness "is" therefore no longer desire). Sexual pleasure is a reflective desire whose object is enjoyment. "The pleasure of caressing is transformed into the pleasure of being caressed."[20] Desire as a particular structure of being of being-for-others is then dead; a rupture of contact with the original project results. This failure of desire, which must of necessity come about, can motivate a passage to masochism.

But desire must miss its goal for still another reason. It seeks by means of caresses to impregnate the Other's body with consciousness and freedom; when its goal is reached, however, and the Other's body has been transformed into flesh and incarnated subjectivity, "it is necessary to take this saturated body, to seize it, to enter into it."[21] But the very attempt soon converts the Other's flesh again into body and into a synthetic instrument which I apprehend in terms of its situation. And exactly the same thing is true of my own flesh. The Other's consciousness "which played on the surface of her flesh and which I tried to taste with my flesh, disappears under my sight."[22] With reciprocity incarnation comes to an end. I attempt to take the Other's body but what I obtain is something other than what I wished to take. Sadism can originate from this situation.

Since desire usually founders on one of two reefs, masochism or sadism, "normal" sexuality is commonly designated as "sadistic-masochistic."

MASOCHISM

If I as a lover absorb the Other and yet leave his freedom untouched (so that I may become what I have always longed to become, being-in-and-for-itself), fail to have him ground and justify my being-there; I may then turn to masochism and project having myself absorbed by the Other, losing myself in his subjectivity, and thereby ridding myself of my own subjectivity. I would in this way become not being-in-and-for-itself but at the very least an in-itself *grounded* on the Other's freedom; I would be able to rest upon the Other. And since I experience my being-as-object as shame (I am ashamed of being an object for the Other), in masochism I love my shame as the sure sign of my objectivity. The Other must desire me as an object worthy of desire; for that reason I make myself in my shame into a desirable object.

Masochism is the assumption of guilt; I am guilty of consenting to my absolute alienation, and I confer guilt on the Other by causing him to miss my freedom. I do not attempt "to fascinate the Other by means of my objectivity but to cause myself to be fascinated by my objectivity-for-others."[1] But it is impossible for me to apprehend or to be fascinated by my self-as-object, such as it is for the Other. The harder I try to enjoy my objectivity, the more conscious I become of my subjectivity. The masochist tends to use the Other as an object and to transcend him toward his own objectivity (for example, he may pay someone to whip him). But in the process his subjectivity is unwittingly freed. Masochism is in principle doomed to failure, for it is a "vice" and every vice is in principle a love of failure.

SADISM

Sadism is consciously contrived and therefore abortive and insatiable desire. The for-itself apprehends itself as engaged and persists in its search, but it has forgotten the nature and aim of its engagement.

The sadist has emptied his desire of its trouble, reapprehended his flesh as body, and resumed his perpetual flight before his own facticity. It is possible that he simply can not realize his true state.

As in the case of desire, the sadist seeks to possess the Other as incarnated transcendence. For this reason it is not possible for him to incarnate the Other by means of his own incarnation and the caresses associated with it. He must therefore use the Other's body as "a tool to make the Other realize an incarnated existence. Sadism is an effort to incarnate the Other through violence, and this incarnation 'by force' must be already the appropriation and utilization of the Other."[1] At the same time the sadist enjoys his own nonincarnation. He enjoys having the Other's freedom imprisoned in the Other's flesh while his own is free. That is why the sadist hurts the Other, for in pain "facticity invades consciousness, and ultimately the reflective consciousness is fascinated by the facticity of the unreflective consciousness."[2] There is indeed an incarnation through pain.

The sadist through the pain that he causes robs the flesh of the grace which veiled it. The flesh appears as flesh and its facticity absorbs the Other's freedom. The sadist aims at destroying grace. He wants to make the Other's flesh appear, to seize upon the Other's freedom. He manipulates the Other's body and uses it as a tool to cause the Other's flesh to appear. "The ideal of the sadist will therefore be to achieve the moment when the Other will be already flesh without ceasing to be an instrument, flesh to cause the birth of flesh, the moment at which the thighs, for example, already offer themselves in an obscene expanding passivity, and yet are bent so as to make the buttocks stick out in order in turn to incarnate them."[3]

Since the sadist seeks to appropriate rather than to stifle the Other's freedom, he forces the Other through torture or threats to beg for mercy, to humiliate himself, to deny what he holds most dear. The Other's freedom must freely identify itself with the tortured flesh: "The body is wholly flesh, panting and obscene. . . . This distorted and heaving body is the very image of a broken and enslaved freedom."[4]

At this moment, however, sadism is confronted by failure. The sadist does not know what to do with the panting body. He has brought its absolute contingency to light and can find no other use for it. I can at the very most incarnate myself in turn and place myself once more "on the level where flesh is revealed to flesh in its entire 'fleshiness,' "[5] which is lost as soon as I use it as a tool. Thus sadism again gives way to desire as unsated desire gave way to sadism. Through "physical possession" a synthesis of sadism and desire is given. "The tumescence of sex manifests incarnation, the fact of "entering into" or of being "penetrated" symbolically realizes the sadistic and masochistic attempt to appropriate."[6] But even this attempt in the end miscarries, for sexual pleasure kills both desire and sadism without satisfying either.

Besides, the sadist is doomed to failure for the reason that the Other's freedom is fundamentally unattainable. The sadist can influence this freedom only to the extent that it is a mere property of the Other and not to the extent that it actually "is" the Other.

HATE

Hate wills the Other's death. Hate owes its origin to the knowledge that I am incapable of diminishing, directing, or dominating the Other's freedom. For as soon as I try to influence the Other, his freedom is transformed from a living expression of his being into nothing more than an objective property of his being, for something essential into something accidental. Indeed, I am guilty toward the Other because by my upsurge in his world I unwittingly confer on him a new dimension of being, namely that of being-for-others (I am in this instance the Other).

The one who hates therefore gives up using the Other as the tool with which he might recover his objectivity, his own being-in-itself. For this end could be accomplished only with the help of a living freedom, and a tool has no freedom. The one who hates seeks unlimited freedom; he wishes to get rid of his being-as-object-for-others (which he can never apprehend) and to eradicate his dimension of alienation (that is, the condition of being something "for" the Other). He projects "the realization of a world in which the Other does not exist."[1] That is why he hates, not a property, but the very existence of the Other. He leaves intact the Other's freedom and wishes to bring about its total destruction. For he hates to be put in a state in which he is subject to the Other's freedom, as when he receives or is forced to accept a favor. As an Arabic proverb puts it, "Whoever takes a gift will lose his life."

Hate toward a certain man is actually hate toward all other men. When I work toward the death of an Other, I wish to destroy the principle of the existence of all others. Through hate I attempt to suppress the enslavement which comes to me through others and win back my unconditional freedom.

But hate is doomed to failure, for even if I nihilate the Other, I can not erase the fact that he has been. "Immediately my being-for-others by slipping into the past becomes an irremediable dimension of myself,"[2] and for it I am all the worse. I can no longer free myself from the Other even though previously I could, at least temporarily (by looking at him and making him my object). "What I was for the Other is fixed by the Other's death, and I shall irremediably be it in the past .... The Other's death constitutes me as an irremediable object exactly as my own death would do."[3]

71

INFERIORITY

"The inferiority complex is a free and global project of myself as inferior before others; it is the way in which I choose to assume my being-for-others, the free solution which I give to the Other's existence, that insuperable scandal."[1] Even when I assert that I am ugly or dumb, I am anticipating my possibilities. In the case of ugliness, for example, what is meant is "the apprehension of the coefficient of adversity which is presented by women or by society to my enterprises,"[2] and which I can apprehend only through the free choice that I make of my possibilities.

Inferiority is not apprehended but lived and felt. It is nonthetic consciousness. It is but a means through which we make ourselves similar to a *thing* and is accordingly related to masochism. Once it has been chosen, however, "it must be lived in accordance with the *nature* which we confer on it by this choice—*i.e.*, in shame, anger, and bitterness."[3]

We can choose a field in which we are inferior in comparison to others only "if this choice implies the reflective *will* to be superior there," for otherwise inferiority could neither be suffered nor recognized. Such a will is therefore in bad faith, for it denies its true end and construes as motives false psychic objects.

I can free myself from my inferiority complex only through a radical modification of my original project. Such a modification can not be the result of suffering and shame occasioned by inferiority, for these feelings are designed to make me realize my project of inferiority. It is necessary on the contrary that the modification be freely chosen.

FACTICITY

Man never exists wholly "for himself" alone but always in a situation which he has not chosen and which is nevertheless his situation. Man is as he is, he "happens to be" (Latin *contigit,* hence man is "contingency"), and with respect to him just as with respect to a house, a tree, or a coffee cup, we can ask, "Why is this particular existent constituted in this way and not in another?"

We emerge in the world but can in no way justify our upsurge or even found our own being-in-the-world. Hence the original contingency of the for-itself. We take upon ourselves this contingency; it is a characteristic of our existence. It stems from the purely contingent being of the thing (which has being-in-itself) which we *also* are, and from the nihilation of the in-itself through the for-itself. "This perpetually evanescent contingency of the in-itself which, without ever allowing itself to be apprehended, haunts the for-itself and reattaches it to being-in-itself—this contingency is what we shall call the *facticity* of the for-itself."[1] A particular aspect of my facticity is the place where I engage myself and act.

Facticity makes possible the assertion that a person *is*, that he *exists*, apart from his state of being and his properties. It

73

can not be apprehended since every act of apprehension brings into play the nonthetic consciousness and because everything conscious reflects the changes imposed on it by the structure of consciousness. For this reason I myself can never see how I am "in fact." "In fact" I possess the contingency of a datum. At the same time, however, I am nonthetically conscious of my facticity, my groundlessness. I feel that I am there *for nothing*, as something *de trop*.

"The for-itself *exists in fact*; that is, its existence can not be identical with a reality engendered in conformity to a law, nor can it be identical with a free choice. And among the factual characteristics of this 'facticity'—*i.e.*, among those which can neither be deduced nor proven but which simply 'let themselves be seen'—there is one of these which we call the existence-in-the-world-in-the-presence-of-others."[2]

There is also a facticity of freedom, namely the *fact* that freedom is a running away from the fact. "Freedom is indispensable to the discovery of my facticity. I learn of this facticity from all the points of the future which I [freely] project; it is from the standpoint of this [freely] chosen future that facticity appears to me with its characteristics of impotence, of contingency, of weakness, of absurdity."[3]

But without facticity there would be no freedom, for there would be nothing for freedom to nihilate and choose, and without freedom "facticity would not be discovered and would have no meaning."[4]

THE PHENOMENON

The appearance of a thing refers to the total series of all possible appearances (an infinite series, of course) of this—finite—thing; it does not refer to some reality hidden under the surface of things. "The being of an existent is exactly what it appears." [1]

The appearance of the *phenomenon* is what it is "absolutely, for it reveals itself as it is."[2] It is "*absolutely indicative of itself*."[3]

Force, for example, is nothing other than the totality of its effects, and electricity is nothing other than the totality of the psysical-chemical processes which manifest it. A physical fact is the synthetic unity of its manifestations. To the extent that we are able to consider the works of a poet as the totality of the manifestations of his person, these works "are" the total series of appearances of his genius.

The appearance of a thing "is" its essence, and the essence of an existent "is the manifest law which presides over the succession of its appearances."[4] Essence is the concatenation of appearances and is itself an appearance.

"The appearance is not supported by any existent different from itself; it has its own being."[5]

THE BODY

Man's body is that which was still a thing when the thing gained consciousness. The body is the viewpoint from which man considers the world—and in addition a viewpoint which came about purely by chance. Besides, man is conscious of his body as one of the structures of his consciousness; body is consciousness of body.

My body is a sign of my facticity. My being-there is first of all my existence as body in the midst of the world, in the midst of things. To be sure, the "look" rather than my body is the instrument or the cause of my relation to others, but it is my body that gives meaning to this relation and sets on it certain limits. "It is as body-in-situation that I apprehend the Other's transcendence-transcended, and it is as body-in-situation that I experience myself in alienation for the Other's benefit."[1]

Through physical pain we can most readily become conscious of man's contingency, though consciousness of body as body is never wholly obliterated but always present to some degree.

This ever-present consciousness of body, though unsavory, is the taste that I always "have." My body always reveals to my consciousness a slight but irradicable nausea which is at the base of all specific feelings of nausea which I experience. Here we are dealing with metaphysical nausea in the presence of things. Things are self-confident, independent, complete, and many-sided to the point of disgust—and they are forever multiplying.

GRACE

The graceful body reveals freedom. The graceful act possesses the exactness and purposiveness of a machine, but at the same time it also possesses the unpredictability of something psychic. For the graceful body appears as something psychic in situation, and whatever is psychic is for the observer always unpredictable. The movements executed by the graceful body seem to be grounded on an aesthetic necessity created by its perfect adaptation to its function. Each movement of the graceful body is understandable in the light of what has already elapsed and of the goal that is to be realized. The movements that have not yet been accomplished are of course not predictable even though we are convinced that they will also appear as necessary and adapted. "It is this moving image of necessity and of freedom (as the property of the Other-as-object) which, strictly speaking, constitutes grace."[1] The graceful act appears as if summoned and it seems to be produced by the appeal that justifies its existence.

Grace has the power to conceal the body's facticity. For instance, the nudity of the flesh is present but can not be seen. "The most graceful body is the naked body whose acts inclose it with an invisible garment while entirely disrobing its flesh, while the flesh is totally present to the eyes of the spectators."[2]

The opposite of gracefulness is obscenity.

THE OBSCENE

The obscene is the opposite of grace. "The obscene appears when the body adopts postures which entirely strip it of its acts and which reveal the inertia of its flesh."[1] A fat rump that waddles involuntarily, for example, is obscene because it is revealed as an unjustifiable facticity. It "exhibits a super-abundant facticity in relation to the effective presence which the situation demands. This revealed flesh is specifically obscene when it is revealed to someone who is not in a state of desire and *without exciting his desire*."[2]

THE HOLE

The hole is something which longs to be filled. The small child is drawn as if by magic to holes. He can not restrain himself from putting in his finger or his whole arm. He makes a symbolic sacrifice of his body to cause the void to disappear and a plenitude of being to exist. The fundamental tendency of human beings to stop up holes persists throughout life, symbolically and in reality. And only from this standpoint can we understand why the feminine sex is obscene. It is obscene because it is a hole and because it sends out an appeal for a plenitude of flesh. A woman also senses her condition as such an appeal, such an enticement. Thus every hole becomes something obscene because it "is an obscene expectation."[1]

THE SITUATION

I apprehend my freedom only to the extent that it reflects the ends that I have chosen. My being is always directly "in situation" in the midst of projects which I am about to realize. All these projects may be traced back to a master plan, to the fundamental project of myself through which I project myself toward my basic possibilities. This fundamental project is to determine that there are values, requirements, expectations, and that at least for me there is a world.

The structures of the situation are my place, my body, my past, my position, my fundamental relations to others. In the situation I order brute things in accordance with my project. I confer upon them meaning and significance. A prohibition established by another man will be binding or not binding on me, depending on my fundamental project. The same is true of a command. "The situation, the common product of the contingency of the in-itself and of freedom, is an ambiguous phenomenon in which it is impossible for the for-itself to distinguish the contribution of freedom from that of the brute existent."[1]

To be sure in a complex situation the coefficient of adversity and utility does not depend solely on the place from which I discover things but also on the particular potentiality of instruments and complexes of instruments. "The abrupt transformation or the abrupt appearance of another instrument can contribute to a radical change in the situation"[2] (a flat tire, for example) and consequently to a reversal of my plans—but not of my fundamental project, of course, which made it possible for the reversal to occur. "Situation and motivation are really one."[3]

My concrete situation is made up of three layers of reality: instruments *already* meaningful (a railroad station, a telephone, a work of art, an induction notice); the meaning I *already* have (my nationality, my race, my appearance); and finally the Other, who is the prime mover and center of reference of the meanings I have *already* brought to light. There arises a paradoxical situation: "I, by whom meanings come to things, I find myself engaged in an *already meaningful* world which reflects to me meanings which I have not put into it."[4] Everything which freedom undertakes always has "one face which freedom will not have chosen, which escapes it and which for the Other will be pure existence."[5] Here we are dealing with a constitutional weakness of freedom.

Since I exist only in situation and since the Other's existence is a *factum*, I create through my free choice of myself a situation which entails the existence of the Other and which in addition is always characterized by the fact that it is always there as a structure-in-itself (that is, as an object that is alienated from me) "for the other."

The situation can not be called subjective, for "it is neither the sum nor the unity of the *impressions* which things make on us. It is *the things themselves* and myself among things. . . . It betrays my facticity, that is, the fact that things simply *are there* as they are without the necessity of being otherwise and that I *am there* among them."[6] Nor can the situation be called objective. It reflects to the for-itself the freedom through which things acquire meaning. That the situation can be neither subjective nor objective results from the fact that it is not an object to be understood by a subject but a *"relation of being* between a for-itself and the in-itself which the for-itself nihilates."[7]

Hence the subject is *nothing* other than his situation. Moreover, the totality of things within the situation (*there is* never anything other than things) is nothing other than this situation. The situation is "the organized totality of the being-there, interpreted and lived in and through being-beyond."[8] This being-beyond through which the situation is nihilated is the same as my own project which goes beyond (transcends) the situation. And since I am constantly projecting myself away from a concrete situation, the outcome of my project will be simple or complicated, depending on the situation. This means, however, that I am either simple or complicated, according to whether I need a simple or a complicated project "to master" the situation.

Since the situation is present only to the extent that it is lived, we can not compare the situations of different men. "Each person realizes only one situation—*his own.*"[9]

"It is because freedom is condemned to be free—*i.e.*, can not choose itself as freedom—that there are things; that is, a plenitude of contingency at the heart of which it is itself contingency. It is by the assumption of this contingency and by its surpassing that there can be at once a *choice* and an organization of things *in situation*; and it is the contingency of freedom and the contingency of the in-itself [that is, of things] which are expressed *in situation* by the unpredictability and the adversity of the environment. Thus I am absolutely free and absolutely responsible for my situation. But I am never free except *in situation.*"[10]

The situation is "the *single countenance* which the world turns toward us as our unique and personal chance."[11]

WILL AND PASSION

The will is free and accordingly possesses "negativity and the power of nihilation."[1] It possesses the autonomy of freedom. It is not the sole or even the privileged manifestation of freedom, but every event in the being-there of the for-itself is such a manifestation.

The will "is posited as reflective decision in relation to certain ends. But it does not create these ends. It is rather a mode of being in relation to them: it decrees that these ends will be reflective to them: it decrees that these ends will be reflective and deliberative."[2] Passion, though it may posit the same ends as the will, proceeds with less deliberation in choosing the means and methods to be employed. The ends are in each instance chosen by freedom, and my being is defined by my ultimate ends. "It is therefore the positing of ultimate ends which characterizes my being and which is identical with the sudden thrust of the freedom which is mine. And this thrust is an *existence*."[3] It has in itself nothing that relates to an essence of property. "Freedom is nothing but the *existence* of our will or of our passions insofar as this existence is the nihilation of facticity." [4]

Since they are posited by freedom, we have only to choose a type of conduct with respect to ends and to decide whether to act by volition or by passion. This decision is mine and mine alone. External circumstances can not prevent me from deciding, for they are my situation, that is, an expression of my freedom. Strictly speaking, there is nothing for the will to decide, for causes and motives have only the weight which my free production of the end and the act to realize it confers upon them. Everything is decided ("the chips are down")[5] before the will can take an active part. If I do actually deliberate, this is because it is part and parcel of my original project or "intention" (which is itself freedom, but which lies deeper than freedom of will) to clarify my motives of conduct by means of deliberation rather than by passion or simply by action. There can be no struggle between will and passion.

Actually it is not enough to will; it is necessary to will to will. In contrast to this act of willing, there is an intention "of losing consciousness in order to do away with the formidable world."[6] Here we have to do with magical behavior. The will, on the other hand, seeks through rational or technical means to solve the problem of organizing the world propitiously for me through rational or technical means. By resorting to the magical or the technical conduct I discover a magical or a technical world. My conduct will depend on my original project and consequently on whether my free project gives to itself technical, emotional, or rational existence. I exist as fearful or courageous, depending on whether I put my freedom in my fear or in my courage. For both I am responsible, for I can be whichever I have chosen. "All my 'modes of being' manifest freedom equally since they are all ways of being my own nothingness."[7] In other words, they are all ways of being what I (still) am not but have to be.

The will can make resolutions which are contrary to fundamental ends. For these resolutions are reflective and therefore subject to error. The reflective consciousness aims at constructing psychic objects in terms of which the will can be organized; in reality, however, these objects are only plausible (all objects are only plausible).

The voluntary act is distinguished from the spontaneous act in that it is an unreflective consciousness of causes.

"The ideal of the will is to be an 'in-itself-for-itself' as a project toward a certain end. This is evidently a reflective ideal and it is the meaning of the satisfaction which accompanies a judgment such as, 'I have done what I wished to do.' "[8]

CAUSE AND MOTIVE

"By cause we mean the *reason* for the act; that is, the ensemble of rational considerations which justify it."[1] It is synonymous with the objective apprehension of a situation in terms of the possibilities which it affords for attaining a particular end.

"The motive, on the contrary, is generally considered as a subjective fact. It is the ensemble of the desires, emotions, and passions which urge me to accomplish a certain act."[2]

The cause is a matter of fact objective, but it is revealed only to a for-itself (through which "there is" a world) which chooses itself in this or that particular way and by so doing makes its own individuality. The instrumental implications of the instrumental-things around us will be revealed in no other way. "In a word the world gives counsel only if one questions it, and one can question it only for a well determined end."[3] Though the cause does not determine the action, it "appears only in and through the project of an action."[4] This project is the motive. Consciousness is always apprehended as engaged, and this "apprehension implies a practical knowledge of the motives of the engagement or even a thematic and positional explanation of these causes."[5]

An inactive motive slips into the past and blends in with "what I have to be in the form of the 'was.'"[6] Such a motive can act only if it is *recovered*; in itself it is without force."[7] I decide the meaning of my earlier motives, recovering or rejecting them as I project myself toward new ends. "Past motives, past causes, present motives and causes, future ends, all are organized in an indissoluble unity by the very upsurge of a freedom which is beyond cause, motives, and ends."[8]

The upsurge of the for-itself causes there to be a world, in the same way the projection of the for-itself toward an end causes there to be a certain objective structure of the world "which deserves the name of cause in the light of this end."[9] A consciousness which projects itself—more or less passionately—toward an end is a motive, and it reveals at the same time that the world "is organized into causes."[10] The motive is the apprehension of the cause. Cause, motive, and end "are the three indissoluble terms of the thrust of a free and living consciousness which projects itself toward its possibilities and makes itself defined by these possibilities."[11]

CONCRETE

"A totality which can exist by itself alone"[1] is concrete. Things are concrete. Consciousness is not concrete, for it exists only as consciousness of something. The phenomenon is not concrete, for it must appear to consciousness in order to exist. "The concrete can be only the synthetic totality of which consciousness, like the phenomenon, constitutes only moments."[2]

Man-in-the-world, in the specific union of man with the world which we call being-in-the-world, is concrete. A host of abstractions can never constitute a concrete entity. Men, the world, and the relation which unites reveal to us men-in-the-world.

THE QUESTION

Every question is a bridge between two non-beings, namely, the non-being of knowing (if I knew, I would not need to ask) and the possibility of non-being in the interrogative phenomenon. For in principle every question can elicit an answer: no, nothing, no one, never, etc. Furthermore, every question implies the existence of a truth and consequently of a third non-being, the non-being of the being that is incompatible with the truth. Non-being therefore conditions the question and limits the answer, for everything that is appears on the basis of what it is not. "Being is *that* and outside of that, *nothing*."[1]

Every question anticipates a revelation of being and assumes that the questioned being will reveal a non-being. Every question therefore envelopes a prejudicative comprehension of non-being.

Every question makes the given into a simple presentation which fluctuates between being and non-being. The questioner frees himself from causality, through which a positive cause produces a positive effect. He takes a nihilating step backwards (a nihilating process has no cause and derives its source from itself), effects a kind of nihilating withdrawal from the given and establishes a neutral interval between being and non-being. At the same time he breaks away from the clutch of being and carves out the possibility of holding as possible non-being.

The question admits into the world negativities, that is, real beings in whose internal structure negation is enveloped as a necessary condition of their presence. Not only can these beings be judged; they can also be questioned, feared, attacked, detested. Such a negativity is the state.

VALUE

Only what my freedom recognizes as valuable exists as a value. A value is revealed only to an active freedom, not to a contemplative intuition which would apprehend it as an object. The being of a value is constituted by the demands which it makes upon me and which in turn exist only to the extent that I acknowledge their existence. My freedom is the sole foundation of values. "My freedom is anguished at being the foundation of values while itself without foundation. It is anguished in addition because values, due to the fact that they are essentially revealed to a freedom, can not disclose themselves without being at the same time 'put into question,' for the possibility of overturning the scale of values appears complementarily as *my* possibility. It is anguish before values which is the recognition of the ideality of values,"[1] that is, the recognition of the fact that values have in themselves nothing objective.

I have no defense against a value, for it is my freedom that invests the value with being. I alone have to realize the meaning of the world and my own existence. Nothing can justify my action and nothing can excuse the "mistakes" that I make.

"Value is the *lack* in relation to which the for-itself determines its being as a *lack*. By the very fact that the for-itself exists, as we have seen, value arises to haunt its being-for-itself."[2] The result is that the for-itself chooses and seeks to attain what it lacks and what therefore appears to it as value. What it lacks is the in-itself that might serve as its own foundation. But such an end is unattainable. Consciousness is accordingly a "missing synthesis" of consciousness and being-in-itself in the form of value.

Values are not transcendental givens, independent of human subjectivity. It is wrong to tranfer the quality of "desirable" from the ontological structure of human reality to the simple material reality of things. It is wrong "to cause the symbolic values of things to be drunk in by their empirical idiosyncrasy as ink by blotter."[3] It is a mistake to posit the desired object in itself as a desirable irreducible. By making this mistake, man hides from himself the free project which he is, he blindly pursues being, "he makes himself such that he is *waited* for by all the tasks placed along his way. Objects are mute demands, and he is nothing in himself but the passive obedience to these demands."[4] By fleeing, he has left behind his own freedom and has put himself in bad faith.

BELIEF

The being of belief is consciousness of belief. "To believe is to know that one believes, and to know that one believes is no longer to believe."[1] Belief is something which questions its own being, that can actually manifest itself only by denying itself. To believe what one believes and to be what one is are ideals of being-in-itself and therefore unattainable. "Every belief is a belief that falls short; one never wholly believes what one believes."[2] We must know something of our belief in order to believe, and knowledge destroys belief. The man in bad faith uses this self-destruction of the fact of consciousness to his advantage by proclaiming the unattainable belief as *his* belief. His inability to believe that he is courageous (while he is in reality cowardly) does not discourage him since every belief involves something basically impossible.

GOOD FAITH

Good faith requires that man be for himself only what he is, that he not delude himself. This means that the principle of identity would have to be applied. He would have to possess being-in-itself in order to be in good faith (the opposite of being in bad faith). In reality, however, man must be able to be what he (still) is not.

Man can not "be" what he is, for he has consciousness and can not exist other than as consciousness of being. The most that can be said is that man has the task of making himself what he is. But if this is our constant task, what "are" we? Man "is" what society requires of him, he plays for society the role which he has been assigned and which he has assumed or had to assume. And he plays this role primarily to himself. Of course man "is" never exactly what a table or a glass "is." He is rather what he "has to be" but "is" not yet completely. He is for others and for himself only a representation and can "be" only in representation. "But if I represent myself as him, I am not he; I am separated from him as the object from the subject, separated *by nothing*, but this nothing isolates me from him. I can not be he, I can only play at *being* him; that is, imagine to myself that I am he. And thereby I affect him with nothingness."[1] To be in good faith, to be oneself, means therefore to make the attempt to play a representative role ("the" honest merchant, "the" typical family man, "the cunning criminal). For others and for myself I am "in the mode of *being what I am not.*"[2]

"I can not say either that I *am* here or that I *am* not here, in the sense that we say 'that box of matches *is* on the table': this would be to confuse my 'being-in-the-world' with a 'being-in-the-midst-of-the-world.' "[3] In other words, my being as subject in my world would be confused with my being as thing in the world of things common to all men.

The ideal of good faith can not be realized, therefore, for its being contradicts the structure of human consciousness. "Having" to be what I am implies that I am *not* originally what I am. But I can not work toward becoming a being-in-itself, and I am well aware of this fact. I know that I can not constitute myself as an object formed by one link in the causal chain. A penal sentence is always directed at a crime that no longer exists.

"The man who confesses that he is evil has exchanged his disturbing claim to "being 'freedom-for-evil' for an inanimate character of evil,"[4] which he can "objectively" condemn. In his striving toward sincerity he therefore constitutes himself as a thing in order to escape the condition of a thing and in order to derive a merit from his sincerity by condemning his character of evil. He is not in good faith but in bad faith. In the last analysis, however, the goals of sincerity and bad faith are not too different. Basically, "so far as my being is concerned, there is no difference between being and non-being."[5]

BEING

Being is what is common to existents. It is the ever present foundation of existents. Many different things are true but there is only one truth. Truth is the being of true things in so far as they are true.

Since being manifests itself in some way to all men, there must be a manifestation of being and therefore a phenomenon of being. Immediately the question arises: might this phenomenon of being be identical with the being of the phenomena which appear to me through things?

Being is not, as Hegel supposed, a moment of the object, one structure beside others: it is rather the condition of all moments and structures. In a particular object we can always distinguish qualities, and proceeding from these, we can determine an essence which they imply. But being is neither a quality nor the meaning of the object. If we strip the object of all its qualities, nothing of being remains. Being is not only the being of the object but also the being of its qualities. Being "is."

The phenomenon of being is an appeal to being; it requires a transphenomenal foundation. Being surpasses the knowledge that we have of it and at the same time provides the basis for our knowledge. Transphenomenal being is the being of the knowing subject. But the law of knowing in the subject is to be conscious.

An object is revealed through the synthesis of the subjective *i*mpressions that I have of it. The object itself is the transcendent boundary, and at the same time the foundation and the goal, of this synthesis.

The existent can always be transcended by consciousness, not toward the being of consciousness but toward the meaning of this being. The meaning of the being of an existent is the phenomenon of being. And this meaning has "a being, based on which it manifests itself."[1]

The being of phenomena is distinct from the being of consciousness. The being of phenomena has the mode of being of being-in-itself; it can be derived neither from something possible, nor from something necessary, nor from another being; it is superfluous (*de trop*). In contrast, the being of consciousness has the mode of being of a degraded being-in-itself, which we call being-for-itself.

The being of phenomena is uncreated but is not—like consciousness—its own cause (*causi sui*). It is in itself. "This means that it does not refer to itself as self-consciousness does. It is this self. It is itself so completely that the perpetual reflection which constitutes the self is dissolved in an identity."[2] Being is what it is, whereas being-for-itself is what it is not but has to be.

NOTHINGNESS

"Nothingness is not."[1] It has no being; furthermore it is the absence of any being. Yet it is necessary, for without nothingness there would be nothing as being; there would be things but there would be no conscious existence. Because nothingness resides in man—and only in man—he can never be identified with himself; he is always separated from himself by nothingness. Because man has nothingness within himself, he can deny the world wholly or partially. This nothingness separates his past from his present; it is a structure of the consciousness which he himself is. It makes him independent of his own past. Because man can say now he is free. One who can not refuse is a slave. If a man can put himself outside being-in-itself, it is because he is not this being and can negate it. Negation has the capacity to nihilate an existent. By nihilation is meant the process through which the for-itself causes a certain existent to emerge from the background of the undifferentiated thing-complex by attributing to the existent a signification (a name, a meaning, a purpose), thereby transcending it and thrusting it back into non-being—for the existent in question ceases to exist as such and continues to exist only insofar as it represents this signification.

Being does not proceed from nothingness; on the contrary, nothingness is logically subsequent to being: nothingness posits being in order to deny it. The total disappearance of being would not be the advent of the reign of non-being, but on the contrary the concomitant disappearance of nothingness. *Non-being exists only on the surface of being.*"[2]

Non-being is forever there, in us and outside us. Being is haunted by non-being, but non-being appears only where being might be expected. Because the physicist expects nature to confirm his hypothesis, the reverse may occur. In other words, non-being can appear only if it has previously been posited as a possibility. Each existent in a given setting must emerge from the ground of other existents which my very expectation has fused into an undifferentiated complex only to be robbed of its individuality and nihilated as soon as I determine that is "is not" the object of my expectation. If the existent which I seek does not emerge, it persists as a nothingness on a ground of nihilation. The expectation of an existent makes possible its absence. Non-being does not come to things through a negative judgment; "it is the negative judgment, on the contrary, which is conditioned and supported by non-being."[3]

Nothingness must be given if there is to be negation and negative judgments. There must be negation in order for us to be able to ask questions, and especially to question being. But nothingness can not be produced by being, for being is wholly positive. Nothingness must be given inside being, "in the heart of being—like a worm."[4]

Nothingness does not nihilate, as Heidegger supposes, for in order to do this it would have to possess being. It does not have its own being; it has only a borrowed being, namely the being of the existent that it was but no longer is. "Nothingness does not nihilate itself; nothingness 'is nihilated.' "[5]

Nihilation can be accomplished not only by being-in-itself (the being of phenomena) but only by an existent whose being encloses the nothingness of being: *The being by which nothingness comes to the world must be its own Nothingness.*[6] To put it another way this being can be only man, for only man can ask questions and confront negatives, the only things that can be questioned.

Every destructible, fragile existent carries within its being "a definite possibility of non-being."[7] The revelation of this possibility is effected through man. An object becomes precious or fragile when man posits it as fragile and takes measures to keep it from being destroyed. "The original meaning and aim of war are contained in the smallest building of man."[8]

TRANSCENDENCE

Transcendence is whatever goes beyond every possible experience. A fact is transcendent if it does not "exist," that is, if it is not a *factum* or a tangible thing. For example, when a liar acts as if he were speaking the truth, he pretends to be a truthful character, "but this character, precisely because he *does not exist*, is a transcendent."[1]

Transcendence is presence in the mode of something transcendent; at the same time it is the capacity for transcending something, for refusing to take something for what it is in itself and for surpassing it toward what it is not, such a signification (which I confer upon it).

Man is transcendent, for he goes beyond every possible experience; he is, in Jasper's words, fundamentally more than can be said about him. As Pascal observed, "*L'Homme supasse infiniment l'homme.*" But man is also transcendence for he has the capacity for transcendence. Man transcends each thing as soon as he makes it "his" object, the object of his judgment, knowledge, or act, and in so doing alienates the object itself; he violates its existence by forcing it to turn toward him a certain facet of its existence and neglecting all other facets (aspects). But man can also be transcended, namely by another man who looks at him, passes judgment on him, and thereby makes him his object. A more brutal way to transcend a man and alienate him from himself is to use him as an instrument for attaining a certain goal (for instance, to torture him in order to elicit information).

To the extent that he transcends objects, man fashions them into his "situation," of which he is himself a part. When this man is seen and therefore transcended by the Other, he is transformed, together with his situation, into something objective. The Other confers on him and the things around him a new signification which he does not perceive. He becomes a transcended transcendence.

GOD

"If I turn away from the look as the occasion of concrete proof [of my being seen and therefore of my objectivity] and seek to think *emptily* of the infinite indistinction of the human presence and to unify it under the concept of the infinite subject which is never an object, then I obtain a purely formal notion which refers to an infinite series of mystic experiences of the presence of the Other, the notion of God as the omnipresent, infinite subject *for whom* I exist."[1] "I thereby posit the eternity of my being-as-object and so perpetuate my shame. . . . By the same stroke I *realize* my object-state in the absolute and hypostasize it. The position of God is accompanied by a reification of my objectness. Or better yet, I posit my being-an-object-for-God as more real than my For-itself; I exist alienated and I cause myself to learn from outside what I must be. This is the origin of fear before God."[2]

There is a fundamental human project which aims at breaking away from individuality, casting off being-for-itself, and fusing in "an absolute totalization of itself and of *all* others. This effort at recovering the human totality can not take place without positing the existence of a Third, who is on principle distinct from humanity and in whose eyes humanity is wholly object."[3] The concept of this unrealizable Third is identical with that of the being-who-looks-at and who can never be looked-at, that is, with the idea of God. But God is radical absence, and "the effort to realize humanity as *ours* is forever renewed and forever results in failure."[4] When I say "we" and mean humanity, I am framing an empty concept, "a pure indication of a possible extension of the ordinary usage of the 'Us,' "[5] the indication of a certain concrete experience to be undergone in the *presence* of the-absolute Third, that is, God. The concepts of humanity and God are correlative and mutually inclusive.

The value that presides over the fundamental project of the for-itself is the in-and-for-itself, that is, the ideal of a consciousness which would be the foundation of its own being-in-itself. If this ideal is called God, the fundamental project of human reality is to become God. God represents the supreme end of man's transcendence and therefore "the permanent limit in terms of which man makes known to himself what he is. To be man means to reach toward being God. Or if you prefer, man fundamentally is the desire to be God."[6]

DEATH

Death is an event in human life. The final chord of a melody consists of silence since it looks toward the nothingness of sound which will follow the melody ("the silence which will follow is already present in the resolved chord as its meaning"[1]); but the final chord also belongs to the melody ("without the chord this melody would remain in the air, and this final indecision would flow back from note to note to confer on each of them the quality of being unfinished"[2]). In the same way death, like every boundary, has two faces: one looks toward nothingness and the other toward life.

For most men death means an immediate contact with the non-human. For romantics and for some poets (Rilke, Malraux, and others) death is interiorized and humanized as the end of life. "Man can not longer encounter anything but the human; there is no longer any *other side* of life, and death is a human phenomenon; it is the final phenomenon of life and is still life. . . . Death becomes the meaning of life as the resolved chord is the meaning of the melody."[3] Considered in this light, however, death is not only human; because it is interiorized, it is my own. "It is the phenomenon of my personal life which makes of this life a unique life— that is, a life which does not begin again. . . . Hence I become responsible for *my* death as for my life."[4] Since human existence suffers nothing precisely because it is totally a project and an anticipation (Heidegger), it projects "its own death as the possibility of no longer realizing presence in the world."[5] Thus human-reality is a *"Sein zum Tode,"* (being unto death).

This romantic-idealistic conception of death is untenable. First we should note the absurd character of death. It is not the resolved chord at the end of a melody. Each of us is rather in the situation of "a man condemned to death who is bravely preparing himself for the ultimate penalty, who is doing everything possible to make a good showing on the scaffold, and who meantime is carried off by a flu epidemic."[6] Moreover, I can not—as the romantics suppose— "expect" death (unless I am confronted with a condemnation to death or an incurable sickness). I can expect "only a determined event which equally determined processess are in the act of realizing."[7] I can "expect" [wait for] a scheduled train and at the same time expect it to arrive late. The possibility of my death "is of the same type as the probable delay of the train,"[8] and not of the type of its arrival. My death can not be foreseen and consequently can not be expected. It is not absolutely true that every minute that passes brings me nearer to death. "Perhaps while I am peacefully writing in this room, the state of the universe is such that my death has approached considerably closer; but perhaps, on the contrary, it has just been considerably removed."[9]

"We have, in fact, every chance of dying before we have accomplished our task, or, on the other hand, of outliving it."[10] Chance, which decides the character of our death, can be apprehended only "as the nihilation of all my possibilities, a nihilation which *itself is no longer a part of my possibilities.* Thus death is not *my possibility* of no longer realizing a presence in the world but rather *an always possible nihilation of my possibles."*[11] If Balzac had died before he wrote *Les Chouans,* he would remain for all time the author of a few abominable novels of intrigue.

Through death the whole past of a life is changed to an

unchangeable in-itself. "The meaning of any phenomenon whatsoever in that life is henceforth-fixed not by itself but by this open totality which is the arrested life. This meaning in the primary and fundamental sense is an *absence of meaning.*"[12] A dead life is not meaningful but absurd, for its intrinsic meaning has accidentally acquired finality.

A dead life becomes the property of others. They can preserve it or let it fall into oblivion, that is, kill it a second time. The relation with the dead is in reality an essential structure of being-for-others. We freely decide the fate of the dead; we decide "the meaning of the efforts and the enterprises of the preceding generation whether we resume and continue their social and political attempts, or whether we realize a decisive rupture and throw the dead back into inefficacy."[13] For the dead life, everything has already been decided; it undergoes changes without being in any way responsible for them and without being able to protect itself against them. The one who tries to apprehend the meaning of his impending death will discover that he is the future prey of others. To die is to be condemned to exist only through others.

"Thus we must conclude in opposition to Heidegger that death, far from being my peculiar possibility, is a *contingent fact* which as such on principle escapes me and originally belongs to my facticity."[14] "It is absurd that we are born; it is absurd that we die."[15]

Being finite is in no way related to having to die. Finitude is an ontological structure of the for-itself. "Human reality would remain finite even if it were immortal, because it *makes itself finite* by choosing itself as human. To be finite, in fact, is to choose oneself—that is, to make known to oneself what one is by projecting one-self toward one possible *to the exclusion of others.* The very act of freedom is therefore the creation and assumption of finitude."[16]

My being is not being unto death. "I am not 'free to die,'

but I am a free mortal."[17] "We can neither think of death nor wait for it nor arm ourselves against it; but also our projects as projects are independent of death—not because of our blindness, as the Christian says, but on principle."[18]

SYNOPSIS: SARTRE'S WORLD

"The for-itself appears in the world." Such a statement is typical of Sartre. It embraces three basic concepts.

First the "for-itself." The for-itself is something conscious, something that possesses consciousness. To be sure, we can not visualize anything that fits this description and must be satisfied with the knowledge that Sartre has in mind something conscious, something that possesses consciousness. Indeed, this something has a long life story; but we are not yet ready to let it speak. The most we can say is that the for-itself is something that all men have in common, both quantitatively and qualitatively. It has absolutely nothing to do with a soul, a spirit, or anything like that. We must rather bear in mind that we are dealing with an ontological concept, not with a cognitive or psychological one. It relates not to man's feeling, thinking, or willing but to his being. The question is not, "How does man find his way in the world? How does he adjust himself to the world?" but rather, "What is the nature of man's *being in* the world? What is the nature of the situation *through which* he adjusts himself to the world?" In other words, we are concerned with the existence of man but not with the means through which he exists! The for-itself must therefore be a structural element in man's being.

This for-itself "appears." Just how it appears Sartre does not say. Just how it appears is obviously unimportant. But since the mere mention of an appearance peremptorily posits the question, we must try to determine in some way how it comes about. We say therefore that the for-itself emerges from some sphere in which there is indeed something, but not a conscious something. How the for-itself attains consciousness belongs to its life story, which will later be told. For the moment we must be satisfied with the fact that the for-itself has already acquired consciousness at the time of its upsurge. Incidentally, this upsurge at once reminds us of the English philosopher Samuel Alexander's concept of emergence; here, somehow and somewhere, categories and qualities of things appear in the course of time, yet the different steps in the process are explained. Alexander's concept is worth keeping in mind; perhaps the process under consideration is like the one we experience on awaking. We emerge from somewhere and for a brief instant we seem like conscious things. A moment later everything is completely different and much more complicated; we have a name, a profession, a past, etc.; we are no longer conscious things but men.

The for-itself appears "in the world"; it makes its way into the world; its advent is prepared beforehand. What is this world? Is it the world of things, of stone, plants and animals, of water, clouds and air? These things are founded wholly on themselves, their existence is questioned by nothing, by no one; they are what they are in themselves. That is why we call the totality of things "in-itself." We now are confronted by two things: the (conscious) for-itself and the in-itself, which possesses no consciousness. Since the for-itself appears in the world of the in-itself, there arises between both a relation which can be a bond as well as a contrast. We shall find that it is at the same time both.

The relation between the for-itself and the in-itself results from two circumstances. First, the for-itself through its emergence enters the world of the in-itself and becomes a constituent part of this world. Second, the for-itself brings its consciousness into play and thereby becomes conscious of itself and of its presence in the world of the in-itself. It becomes conscious of the fact that a world of things exists and that it exists among a world of things. Before the upsurge of the for-itself things simply were there; now, however, they have become constituent parts of a consciousness. Consciousness is consciousness of the world and at the same time awareness of the fact that "there is" a world.

This consciousness of the world we call "nonpositional consciousness." The expression signifies that the world is inexpressibly present, so to speak, as a totality whose parts are indistinguishable. Consciousness is aware only of the fact that here "there is" something to see, to hear, to perceive. It does not single out separate elements. We experience the nonpositional consciousness when we are in a stupor. As a matter of fact, however, consciousness is always both positional and nonpositional at the same time. Here the expression "positional" has the signification of "substantiating" or "confirming." In the positional consciousness the for-itself turns toward a definite, particular thing; this is what we call a psychic act. Through the psychic act the thing appears in the consciousness; it changes from a thing to a phenomenon, an appearance. The thing itself, the in-itself, can not enter into consciousness but remains forever outside, unknowable; only the phenomenon corresponding to the in-itself can enter into consciousness.

The upsurge of the for-itself in the world therefore involves both particular things and phenomena. Because this is generally true, people often say thing when they mean phenomenon. It is worth noting that a phenomenon has an infinite number of aspects. A structure that occupies space, for instance, can be viewed from an infinite number of different standpoints and will present to each observer a particular side. Only an observer capable of viewing it from every possible standpoint could discover what the phenomenon is in reality. An individual for-itself must be satisfied with one or with only a few aspects, and throws wide open the gateway to error. The phenomenon consists of a set of colored surfaces, sounds, smells, tactile sensations, etc. But consciousness does not waste its time on such a set of sensory data; rather it immediately goes beyond the phenomenon (it "transcends" the phenomenon) and transforms it into something that it in no way "is," such as a hammer, a table, a house, or the like. The for-itself can not experience the reality of the phenomenon, as we said, because it is never able to apprehend more than a few of its aspects. The for-itself does know, however, what the phenomenon "means." For instance, it may mean "hammer." The for-itself confers this meaning on the phenomenon—just how remains to be seen—and the meaning is valid forever only with respect to the for-itself in question. A stone may have for me the meaning "hammer" whenever a real hammer is not available. Occasionally it may have the meaning "missile." To the signification "hammer" belongs naturally also the meaning of hammer, namely "the act of hammering," and the purpose of the act of hammering, namely "to drive in a nail."

The totality of phenomena is the "world" in the particular sense in which it "is" for the for-itself—as nonpositional consciousness of the world and positional consciousness of phenomena.

The for-itself is something and it is conscious; apart from these considerations, it has still another important characteristic. It is free. Immediately the old question arises: Free from what and free for what? The answer is: Free from contingency and free to do anything. The answer is unsatisfactory and raises other questions. How is it possible that the for-itself is not a link in the chain of causality? Because it engenders nothingness. How it does this Sartre fails to say, but he does say why.

The for-itself brings forth nothingness and brings it into the world in order to be able to "nihilate." To nihilate means to be dissatisfied with the raw existent and to transform it into something that will conform more closely to my intentions. Everything that is transcended, for example, is nihilated. If I shape a slice of bread into a ball, I nihilate the bread; I transform it into non-being and set in its place a new being, that of the ball. At the same time I transcend the bread by surpassing it in the direction of my possibilities and using it to form a ball. I attribute to the bread the new signification of raw material for constructing a ball; that is, I nihilate its old signification of ingredients for providing nourishment.

Nothingness enables the for-itself to isolate itself and separate phenomena from one another. What separates the for-itself from the in-itself? Nothingness. But this nothingness is capable of making the for-itself discover that it is "not" the in-itself. Nothingness opens the possibility of negating or denying a fact. In particular it opens the possibility of breaking the chain of causality; that is, the for-itself can negate its own causal contingency. Since the for-itself is consciousness, and since consciousness is constantly changing with time, the present for-itself is grounded on the past for-itself but is not conditioned by it. But an existent which does not need to be another existent and which is not conditioned by another existent is free. Moreover, the freedom of the for-itself is contingent; it is unfounded and incapable of being provided with a foundation.

If the for-itself is to engender nothingness, then it must bear within itself this nothingness. That is in fact the case. Nothingness lies between the For and the Self. For the for-itself consists, as the name implies, of two parts which are separated from each other by nothing (except the hyphen). If instead of "for-itself" we use the longer expression "in spite of itself," these relations become clearer. The for-itself is not simply there; rather it has a purpose, it shapes itself to suit its purpose, it fashions thoughts concerning itself, it is conscious of itself. The for-itself is no self-contained unity, positive through and through like a thing; on the contrary, it is marked by a cleavage which makes it possible for it to effect a withdrawal from itself and to confront itself directly. The for-itself does not rest in itself but is highly disturbed for the very reason that it *does not* rest in itself like a thing but is full of unrest. What is paradoxical in this situation is that the for-itself does not wish in the least to be in-itself. It maintains on the contrary that it is *not* in-itself. At the same time it wishes to appropriate for itself the mode of being of the in-itself, namely being-in-itself.

The conduct of the for-itself is contradictory, but it is obvious that something is lacking, that the for-itself perceives itself as deficient and seeks to correct its deficiency. In fact, this is the true meaning of freedom. Something through which I identify my deficiency is converted not only into a lack but also into something of value. If follows that value does not exist in its own right but is fixed by the for-itself. What the for-itself lacks, however, is not a particular thing (as I might lack a handkerchief), but a structure that will rule out the appearance of lack. The for-itself therefore desires not an object but itself in the quality of a new, better for-itself. Its striving finds expression in a free project toward a freely chosen end. This end is the mode of being of a for-itself which has along with its own qualities those of the in-itself. This desired mode of being we call being-in-and-for-itself.

Let us note at this point that the upsurge of the for-itself, consciousness of the for-itself, freedom of the for-itself, the choice of the for-itself, and the project of the for-itself must be understood as one and the same process, identical in every respect to the for-itself.

As soon as the for-itself appears in the world, a "situation" arises. The situation comprises all the data which the for-itself must reckon with if it wishes to exist in the world. Although consciousness can transcend phenomena and confer on them a particular signification in terms of the for-itself, at the time of its upsurge the for-itself finds itself in a situation in which almost everything already has a signification whose origin is somewhere else. Still, everything receives from the for-itself a second signification—a private signification, so to speak— and this confusion is in every respect typical of every concrete situation. These private significations are in their totality the face that the for-itself turns to the world. In this face it recognizes itself, for in it significations have their origin.

The concrete situation in which the for-itself finds itself makes possible the free choice of an end and the free project toward this end. The for-itself can choose only what lies within the range of its possibilities; it can only choose what is possible, and this is determined by the situation. It is paradoxical that the for-itself creates the situation by transcending phenomena and selects from the possibilities inherent in the situation an end toward which it can project itself. But man's existence is itself paradoxical, and it is clear that paradoxes must appear everywhere. In any event, we must not minimize the importance of the situation. To it belong not only the home, the family, friends and acquaintances, place of work, the street, the city, etc.

To it belong also the political, economical, and cultural conditions of Germany, Europe, and the world to the extent that they are known to me, to the extent that I make them objects of my reflection, judgment, hopes and fears, and especially to the extent that I allow them in some way to influence me. Choice and project therefore issue from the concrete situation, and at the same time the for-itself (since two identical situations never arise) becomes something individual: a man fused into such a close union with the situation that he must be called man-in-situation. I am this man-in-situation, and through my being-in-situation I am distinguished from other men; my being-in-situation is my individuality.

The for-itself at the same time of its upsurge in the world is confronted by a multitude of things already endowed with meaning, and forced at the outset to accept a situation, for better or for worse. But that is not all. The for-itself must also make the discovery that through its situation it has unwittingly acquired all sorts of significations (European, Catholic, neurotic, etc.) and that it coexists with many others that also have their signification, are also free, and can also choose and project themselves toward ends. Clearly conflicts must arise. The existence of others is perceived by the for-itself as an "unsurpassable scandal."

Still, the ego, that is, the for-itself in situation, needs the Other, and this for a very definite purpose. I doubtlessly know myself best, I can see through myself (Sartre resolutely denies the existence of an unconscious psychic life), and I can never be mistaken concerning myself. I also know, however, that my knowledge of myself is purely subjective. This does not mean that my knowledge is false or must contain an element of falsity. It does mean that my knowledge is valid for me alone. If I am not satisfied by this insight—and people rarely are—I must try to discover not only what I am subjectively but also what I am objectively, factually, actually, in reality. We know immediately that all these expressions point to an observer who can see me "from the outside," and that we give more weight to the way others picture us than to the way we picture ourselves. This results not so much from an innate mistrust of our capacity for judgment as from the intuitive grasping of the fact that we exist not only for ourselves (for in this case the subjective judgment would satisfy us completely) but also for others, and that every being-for-itself corresponds to being-for-others in the same subject.

The observer that I need to discover what I am objectively is the Other. Here it is also worth noting that I can never judge myself objectively; for myself I can never become an object. One who nevertheless acts as if this were possible is practicing self-deception. Only the Other can judge me objectively by making me an object (more exactly; his object). He does this by looking at me. At this moment I become for him a phenomenon and take on all the characteristics of a phenomenon. The most important of these is that I become transcendable. The Other transcends me as he transcends every object to his liking and thereby confers on me a signification which corresponds to *his* intention. Now I can ask him what I signify for him and can discover what I am objectively. My objectivity does not seem absolute, of course, for we have already seen that a phenomenon can be viewed from countless standpoints and that each standpoint of our choosing yields an "objective" picture of the phenomenon. I ought therefore to ask not one Other but several others what I am objectively. If I could ask all others—all who have ever lived and will ever live—I would then discover what I am in an absolute sense, what I am "in itself." The desire to make such a discovery has been so intense throughout time that men have substituted for the (unrealizable) concept "all others" the concept "God" which, though also unrealizable, is more familiar to them because it is closely related to the universal father complex.

But the fact that the Other can see me and make me his object has serious implications. For as soon as I become an object I suffer the loss of my freedom, or more exactly, my freedom is changed from an active agent to a passive quality of the type possessed by all objects. The change is from concrete to abstract freedom. An example drawn from physics will clarify the issue. I observe that when a circuit is switched on, an electric bulb will light up; from this observation I can draw the conclusion that a current is a force that can cause an electric bulb to light up. When I try to pinpoint the difference between "force" and "causing-to-light-up," however, I find that it is purely intellectual; "force" and "causing-to-light-up" are the abstract and concrete aspects of one and the same thing, which we call electricity. In the same way I say that my concrete freedom, which can not be distinguished from its effects, becomes an abstract possibility of manifesting freedom as soon as the Other sees me and makes me his object.

The truth of this is found in daily life. If we are convinced that no one sees us but suddenly discover that someone is looking at us, we undergo a change. Our bearing, our movements, our voices change; even our thinking is no longer the same as before. We describe the situation in this way by saying that the Other irritates us and embarrasses us; we suddenly feel that we are no longer free. The sum and substance of it all is that we really have lost our freedom. In large restaurants one can observe that every patron wishes to sit with his back to the wall and even if possible in a corner. The tables in the center of the restaurants are not chosen, and enterprising restaurateurs for this reason make use of niches, booths, etc. to increase the available wall space. Every patron, though he knows of course that he is seen, wishes to avoid being seen from behind or even from the side since in either instance he would be unable to determine who was observing him and when he was being observed (waiters do not count). If he must be seen, he wishes to be seen from the front in order that he may enjoy the important advantage of being able to look at the one who is looking at him. The result is the well-known duel of looks in which the loser is the one who first looks away, for he is the object.

The other appears before me therefore "as a look." Indeed, if he is not looking at me, he is not an Other; he is only an object of my choice, even though one of particular significance. The Other's look transcends me, makes me his object, and confers on me significations of his choice. As a rule these significations are of no interest to me. I can be indifferent as to whether the Other confers on me the signification "passerby," "man-reading-a-newspaper," or "poor devil." But it is worth noting that I am never *wholly* indifferent. The signification can also be odious ("repulsive creature") or even dangerous ("That's the proprietor, the lout!"). All these significations emanate from the Other's freedom, for only because he is free can he break away from the phenomenon that I am for him and transcend it. These significations are as a rule unknown to me, with the result that the Other's freedom represents for me a danger. How can I protect myself against the danger?

There would be no point in my making the Other an object, for I apprehend only the outside of an object. As soon as I look at the Other he withdraws into an impenetrable shell which hides from me his consciousness and his freedom. His freedom, which he owes to me alone, congeals as a mere possibility of being free. His active freedom eludes me. Never can I possess his freedom conclusively. Besides, the Other can always turn the tables on me and make me his object.

Again we are faced by a paradoxical situation. The Other also figures in the nonpositional consciousness that I have of the world. I know intuitively and with absolute certainty that I also exist in the Other's nonpositional consciousness and that in his positional consciousness I may be a definite person about whom he has formulated a certain opinion. I know further that this opinion is made possible by his freedom, that it represents for me a danger, and that I must try to overpower this freedom. As soon as I initiate my attempt and turn to the Other, however, he shrivels up into something impenetrable, his freedom congealed and beyond my reach. I destroy through my attempt the freedom that I am trying to find.

112

Fundamentally, nothing in this situation can be changed, for it rests on the unchangeable structure-of-being of the for-itself. But its harshness can be tempered and an attempt made to approach the Other's freedom and still leave it intact. The path that leads to the Other's freedom is as old as time: it is love. In love I try not to overpower the Other's freedom but to incorporate it into myself as it is. I try to fuse with the Other and by so doing to make it impossible for him to make me his object. I try to be present in his consciousness as subject and to approach his own freedom confidently. From the outset my attempt is certain to fail, however, for if the Other loves me, I become the object of his love—but only an object, a thing. But I do succeed in approaching his freedom. Theoretically I can never be at the same time both object and subject and consequently never both beloved and lover. Practically, however, both roles are constantly being interchanged so rapidly that they are indistinguishable. Practically it always seems that both lovers have in reality but one soul, one consciousness, one freedom. Still, the situation is indeed perilous, and considerable energy is required to preserve it for an appreciable period of time.

Many other attempts are made to put up a defense against the effect of the Other's freedom. Examples include hate, pride, humility, obedience, indifference, lying, violence, authority. These attempts are also certain to fail, individually and collectively, for the same reason as love; the only difference is that they are more short-lived. Freedom as such is inapprehensible. One can apprehend only that through which freedom is in some way perceptibly symbolized.

We turn back once again to reconsider the for-itself and study its evolution. We had broached the supposition that the for-itself emerges from a sphere in which there is no consciousness. This sphere must be the realm of things, of the in-itself. When and how did the in-itself become the for-itself? Sartre states that the question belongs not to ontology but rather to metaphysics. Ontology could at most indicate the direction which the search for the answer might take. The in-itself rests in itself and is self-sufficient. And there is no reason why this condition should not endure forever. Yet the in-itself is not satisfied with its position. It suffers from its contingency and therefore from the fact that its presence is unfounded and unfoundable. It wishes to found itself, to discover why and for what purpose it is there, to affirm itself. Clearly there is no easy solution. I can take up a position only with respect to something opposite me. There must be an interval between me and that something or an interval must be created. To establish the necessary interval the in-itself absorbed nothingness. The result was that the in-itself was divided into two parts. Between the two parts was a cleavage and in this cleavage there was no in-itself, nothing. Furthermore, the whole in-itself was no longer present; it had given way to and been "degraded" by the for-itself. The use of the expression "degraded" is typical of Sartre. He says that ontologically the in-itself takes precedence over the for-itself and that man is a hapless thing. The in-itself has exchanged its self-sufficiency for the consciousness of the for-itself, and Sartre is of the opinion that the exchange is a poor one. Now the for-itself can indeed say, "I am *not* the in-itself," but this statement is possible only because it bears within it nothingness. The for-itself has brought into the world not only nothingness and the dangerous possibility of negation but also the consequences of both: freedom and along with it human existence.

Everything coheres and is basically the same: having consciousness, having an understanding of non-being, being free, being able to deny, being able to choose. The totality is constantly involved in the existence of man. To his existence belongs also his contribution to the for-itself, for when the in-itself became the for-itself one of its parts remained unchanged; man's body is one proof of the fact that the "itself" is common to both the in-itself and the for-itself. To the extent that man has a body, he exists factually, like a datum. We say that man is afflicted with "facticity," which he simply has to accept. To his facticity belong in addition his past, his situation, the spot where he is standing, etc. But all these factual data in no way circumscribe his freedom. Let us consider the body, for instance, and assume that a man is suffering from the fact that he is weakly and small. What is the origin of the judgment, "I am weakly and small?" Does it result from necessity or does man's freedom play a part? The judgment is doubtlessly based on a comparison. It can mean, "I am weaker and smaller than the average man in my age group." This interpretation would entail no suffering on his part, for the man does not really care how big and strong the average man is. Besides, his freedom has no part in its judgment, which necessarily results from a statistical comparison (presuming that such statistics are accessible). But the original judgment that causes suffering can also mean, "I am weaker and smaller than I would like to be." Here the case is quite different. The condition of the body is not compared with that of the normal or average person but with a freely projected ideal. The man appears to himself as weakly and small. The man envisions himself as weakly and small because he would like to be a famous football player or because he would like to be loved by a beautiful girl who is tall. This means, however, that he freely projects himself toward an end, transcends his body, makes it his object, and confers on it the signification "weakly and small." It is evident that his body could not possibly have *this* signification apart from the project of his becoming a famous player or the lover of a tall girl. It may be objected that everyone probably tells him that he is a weakling. Statistics would have revealed the same thing to him without his being particularly disturbed. What the objective fact that he "is" a weakling *signifies for him*

115

depends on his free project and therefore only on himself. We also know that freedom is not in the least disturbed over whether or not a project can be realized. If I intend to go from Stuttgart to Munich but am detained on the highway by a flat tire, then my freedom would be disturbed by this circumstance if the flat tire could force upon me a certain conduct. We see immediately that it can not, for in itself the flat tire is nothing; it becomes something only when I confer on it a signification. Only the signification matters. Through the affirmation, "That means nothing to me," we effectively change a fact into non-being by nihilating it; this does not prevent the Other from appropriating it and conferring on it a signification.

The free project is also the basis for all activity. To act is to change something. When I do something, I wish to bring about a situation which does not yet exist but which seems to me desirable. I freely project this future situation for the reason that in terms of it the present situation seems to require change, to be in some way deficient. Sartre says, "I judge what exists in terms of the situation that exists." And the same applies to me. I judge myself in terms of the end (for instance, being a football player) toward which I have projected myself—or as Sartre expresses it—my freely chosen end reveals to me who I am. This means, however, that I am not but that I make myself.

We have determined that the for-itself is unsatisfied with the situation in which it finds itself. It is broken apart, split asunder, separated from itself. To be sure, it has nihilated the in-itself in order to become for-itself, but it still misses the placid self-sufficiency of the in-itself. It would like to regain being-in-itself—the mode of being of the in-itself, though in a "degraded" form, the in-itself proper. To be sure, it is not willing to surrender the possibility of founding itself, to suffer the loss of its consciousness (and along with conscious-

116

ness, its freedom). It is obvious that such an end is unrealizable. Being-in-itself and being-for-itself are forever separated; between them stands Nothingness, invincible even in the absence of something to be overcome. A thing is what it is *in itself*: man is what he makes himself be *for himself*; something which would be "in-and-for-itself"—what it is *and* what it must be—is inconceivable. Nevertheless, or perhaps precisely because this is true, man's fundamental project is to achieve the mode of being of the in-and-for-itself. This is obviously what Ernst Weichert had in mind when in his novel *The Simple Life* he made known his ideal: "Joyful hearts, still as stones on the ground, want nothing for themselves."

The fundamental project is supplemented and overlaid by an unforeseeable number of ancillary projects which are constantly recurring and changing, and which make it possible to cope with the vicissitudes of daily life. Sartre stresses the fact that the goals which mark the limits of our projects must be freely chosen and that no one can take from us this choice. If we were *given* an end, by God, for example, it could not appear to us as an end whose meaning is to make known to us who we are but only as an object. To have a signification and a meaning for us, however, the object would have to be transcended by us and therefore made to disappear as non-being. But if transcendence were for some reason ruled out—if the end were posited as something final or insurmountable perhaps—it would be impossible to confer on it a meaning. Weichert probably had this in mind when he wrote, "If we exempt the world from God's love, it takes on a meaning."

Freedom also has a negative side. It exists factually. This means, however, that we are unable not to be free. Even if we chose as an end to lead the existence of a slave with no will of his own (some love relationships are of this type), freedom would be required for our choice, and never would there be a time when we could not revoke the choice. We *must* choose, and if we abstain from choosing, we choose to abstain from making a choice. To put it somewhat dramatically but still not forcefully enough, "We are condemned to be free."

REFERENCES*

THINGS—[1]487, [2]509, [3]509.

IN-ITSELF AND FOR-ITSELF—[1]617, [2]618, [3]619, [4]620, [5]620, [6]620, [7]621, [8]621, [9]621, [10]621, [11]623.

MAN—[1]506, [2]479, [3]519, [4]626, [5]626, [6]259, [7]284, [8]284, [9]284, [10]285, [11]289, [12]292, [13]293, [14]362, [15]363, [16]363, [17]363, [18]364, [19]430, [20]430, [21]453, [22]463, [23]546, [24]477, [25]478, [26]506, [27]507, [28]478, [29]479, [30]488, [31]496, [32]496, [33]498, [34]499, [35]503, [36]503, [37]554, [38]556, [39]556, [40]626, [41]627, [42]627.

CONSCIOUSNESS—[1]li, [2]li, [3]liii, [4]liv, [5]liv, [6]lv, [7]lv, [8]lvi (note), [9]lv, [10]lix, [11]618, [12]lxii, [13]36, [14]62, [15]478, [16]618, [17]241, [18]298.

FREEDOM—[1]28, [2]433, [3]435, [4]438, [5]438, [6]439, [7]439, [8]440, [9]440, [10]441, [11]480, [12]459, [13]461, [14]462, [15]462, [16]462, [17]475, [18]476, [19]479, [20]482, [21]482, [22]483, [23]483, [24]507, [25]485, [26]486, [27]485, [28]487, [29]525, [30]531.

THE OTHER AND HIS LOOK—[1]222, [2]222, [3]226, [4]228, [5]249, [6]244, [7]253, [8]254, [9]255, [10]255, [11]257, [12]259, [13]262, [14]262, [15]263, [16]264, [17]265, [18]267, [19]267, [20]267, [21]267, [22]268, [23]269,

---

* Numbers refer to pages in *Being and Nothingness* (Philosophical Library, 1956), Professor Barnes' translation of Sartre's *L'Etre et le Néant*. Tr.

GOD—[1]281, [2]290, [3]423, [4]423, [5]423, [6]566.

DEATH—[1]531, [2]531, [3]532, [4]532, [5]533, [6]533, [7]535, [8]535, [9]536, [10]536, [11]537, [12]541, [13]543, [14]545, [15]547, [16]546, [17]547, [18]548.

KEY TO SPECIAL TERMINOLOGY

Absurd

Meaningless. Man's existence is absurd since his contingency (*q.v.*) is without justification, and his projects (*q.v.*) are absurd since his ends (*e.g.* his desire to become God) are unattainable.

Anguish

The apprehension of the self as freedom; the realization that my self is separated from my past and my future, with the result that I must continually make choices in the absence of fixed values.

Appearance

The coming into existence, emergence, or upsurge of an object. This is only from the viewpoint of the for-itself since being neither "comes" nor "goes."

Aspect

One of several possible or successive appearances of an object viewed from a particular standpoint by the for-itself.

Bad Faith

Through bad faith we seek to escape our responsible freedom of being-for-itself. We vacillate between transcendence and facticity, refusing to recognize them for what they are or to synthesize them.

Being	While existence is individual and subjective, being is all-embracing and objective. It includes both being-in-itself and being-for-itself.
Being-for-itself	Consciousness conceived as a lack of being, a desire for being, a relation to being. Each for-itself is the nihilation of a particular being.
Being-in-itself	Non-conscious being. The being of the phenomenon. It overflows our knowledge of it; it is a plenitude; we can say only that it is.
Coefficiency of Adversity	Resistance offered by objects to the projects of the for-itself.
Contingency	Facticity, the brute fact of being a particular for-itself.
Dasein	Literally "being-there." The human being considered as a conscious existent.
Datum	A given. An inescapable fact.
Emergence	The coming into existence or upsurge of an object. See "Appearance."
Essence	What has been. Man's past. Each man makes his essence as he lives it.

124

Existence	Concrete, individual being here and now. Existence, which has a subjective quality, always precedes essence.
Facticity	The for-itself's necessary connection with the in-itself and consequently with the world and its own past. The facticity of freedom is the fact that freedom is not able not to be free.
For-itself	By bringing nothingness into the world the for-itself can separate itself from being and judge other things. It exists as a knowing subject.
Freedom	The very being of the for-itself. To be free does not mean to obtain what one has wished but rather to project an end.
In-itself	That which exists independently of us. A non-conscious being.
Instant	The initial and the final term in the choice of a new project of being. Time is not a succession of instants. The instant designates the psychological possibility that the for-itself has of suddenly effecting a rupture in its existence by choosing a new project of being.
Metaphysics	The study of why concrete existents are as they are.
Nausea	The "taste" of the facticity and contingency of existence.

125

Negativity	Types of human activity which do not involve negative judgment but include in their structure negation (e.g. experiences involving absence, interrogation, destruction).
Nihilate	To encase in a shell of non-being by making a nothingness arise between consciousness and its object.
Nothingness	The non-presence of something. Nothingness is supported by being, which it lacks, and is brought into the world by the for-itself.
Objectivity	The quality or state of being an object.
Ontology	The study of being itself, the conditions by which "there is" a world, human reality, etc.
Phenomenon	Being as it appears or is revealed.
Project	Substantive and verb referring to the for-itself's choice of its mode of being. A project is expressed by action directed toward a particular end.
Self-consciousness	Nonthetic or nonpositional self-consciousness, also called unreflective consciousness, is an implicit consciousness of being conscious of an object. Thetic or positional self-consciousness, also called reflective, is the attempt on the part of consciousness to become its own object.

Transcendence	The process through which the for-itself goes beyond or surpasses the given in pursuing its project. By making him an object, I transcend the Other.
Transphenomenal	Referring to the fact that being surpasses and provides a basis for our knowledge of being.